Down the Rabbit Hole:

A Memoir of Abuse, Addiction

and Recovery

by Kate Russell

Down the Rabbit Hole

For Miggie

Down the Rabbit Hole

Table of Contents

1) Who's Your Daddy

2) Choosing to Deny

3) Not So Private Parts

4) Return to Sender

5) The Big Black Babysitter

6) The Life I Wanted vs. the Life I Had

7) Kids? What Kids?

8) Dunkin' Donuts

9) The Common Crash

10) Sick Brains

11) Step 1?

12) My Safe Haven

13) Myself / My Friend

14) Drunken Abuse and Sober Promises

15) Bullied

16) Mom's Typical Overreaction

17) Breakfast Coke

18) Les Miserables

19) Plaster Victim

20) Mommy Dearest

Down the Rabbit Hole

21) Similarities

22) MY Father Knows Best

23) A Peak Inside the Chaos

24) Walking Pneumonia

25) Road Trips

26) The World's Best Ten Year Old Mommy

27) Jaba the Head

28) Egging

29) Lessons

30) Gumma's Back Porch

31) Confiding in the Shower

32) Group

33) Fiddler on the Roof

34) Our Sociopathic Father and Our Suicidal Dog

35) Serial Mom

36) Familial Alienation

37) Fake Diary

38) My 13th Birthday Party

39) Embarrassed of What?

40) Oak Park

41) Child See, Child Do

42) Rageaholic

43) Three Past Drinking Hour

Down the Rabbit Hole

44) Anorexia

45) Self Medicating

46) Busted

47) Divorce Gift

48) Vacationing with a Liar

49) Honestly

50) An Untreated Disease Resurfaces

51) From Rage to Guilt

52) College, Part 2

53) Hot Mess

54) Up, Up and Away

55) Opening Night

56) Moving My Baggage West

57) Pushing

58) The Death of My Best Friend

59) The Death of My Worst Enemy

60) AA Crux

61) Boundary Setting

62) What it's Like Now

Down the Rabbit Hole

Chapter 1 — Who's Your Daddy?

It was the middle of the night, maybe two AM. My father was on the road and my sister, mother and I were living on Bend Lane in the house right next door to Gumma and Da. I was awoken by my mother's screams and a man yelling at her 'not to do this.' It was a startling way to be awoken, but because her screams were directed at someone other than me, I felt relieved. The ruckus was ongoing, a cry for attention. *For Christ's sake, woman, fine - I'll investigate.* I tentatively opened my bedroom door.

I tiptoed out of my room and saw a man with a sandy brown crew cut, wearing a beige members only jacket, standing at the bottom of the stairs.

"Hello, Kate. I'm Siobhan's father," he said.

My mother was sobbing loudly behind her locked bedroom door. The man edged cautiously up the stairs, so as not to scare me.

"I have her picture in my wallet, if you don't believe me," he said, as if that were all the proof I'd need.

Down the Rabbit Hole

"What's going on?" I asked, addressing the larger issue at hand.

"Your mother has taken a bunch of pills and wants to die," he said nonchalantly. He was now far more concerned with my opinion of him than he was with my mother's well-being. "She won't let me call the police because she's afraid they'll take you and Sibby away from her."

She won't let you call the police because they'd find her drunk and on drugs, my good-humored God voice corrected him in my head. I smiled. There was God, holding me, making a joke, letting me know everything was going to be OK.

"Go away, Michael!" my mother shouted through slurred speech. So "Sibby's father" had a name.

"Ok, ok," he said and backed down the stairs slowly.

But I didn't want him to leave. Perhaps, if he stayed, he could rescue me and Sibby from this monster he'd just prevented from killing itself. He had a responsibility to us now! He couldn't just drop a bomb like that on us and leave! What kind of father was he?

Down the Rabbit Hole

My mother threw open her bedroom door and grabbed me in a hug. She reeked of vodka, her face and tip of her nose were bright red, her eyes bloodshot and strewn with tears. So, she looked pretty normal, only she was crying. The most unusual thing so far was that she was hugging me.

"Get out of here, Michael!" my mother yelled again.

He took a beat, then turned and left. My mother broke down in tears again.

"I love you and Sibby so much!" she sobbed. "I never want anything bad to happen to you!"

She didn't realize that *she* was the bad thing that continued to happen to us.

I wondered why, if she had taken "a bunch" of pills as Michael had said, she was still coherent. Another lie for attention. Or her tolerance was so high "a bunch" didn't affect her. Either way, she was alive and I was stuck with her.

Down the Rabbit Hole

I went back to bed and my mother did too. The next day we proceeded as if the previous night hadn't happened. We usually just avoided that kind of awkwardness.

I never brought Michael up to anyone. I found out a few years later that Sibby *and my dad* knew about him. Kudos to Ed for continuing to treat Sibby as if she were his own.

"Eddie isn't your real father," I had heard Denise drunkenly disclose, what I had believed was a lie, to my innocent sister late at night, when she did her best brainwashing.

"Who is, Buddha?" Sibby naively replied.

"... Yes." My mother: full of rage, claiming to have been knocked up by the God of non-violence. Pardon me for saying so, but I don't think she was his type.

Chapter 2 — Choosing to Deny

Several weeks after their first trial separation Denise kicked Ed out of the house again, this time because - ahem - *he* was an alcoholic.

My dad went to live with his parents, and my mother used our alone time to try and convince me that it was *he*, not *she*, that indeed had the drinking problem. She made some good points: he was abusive when he drank, and he did things he did not remember the next day… *But, um, you do those things too,* my wise, 5-year old, inner God voice quipped. I was already too smart to be fooled by her projecting.

My father stayed with his parents for two weeks. He was a fairly new stagehand, and was working on a show in New Haven. Getting home late, after his parents were asleep, he'd drink in order to unwind after his long day. Then he'd do some cocaine so he could stay up longer and drink more.

Ed didn't believe addiction was a "disease." He thought it was a "choice." You can have a few drinks and snort a few lines and then stop, or you can *choose* to get wasted, but it is not beyond your control. You *can* control it. You just *choose* not to.

Down the Rabbit Hole

He was well-behaved for the first thirteen days. Determined to prove that he was not an alcoholic, he tempered his using to only a few drinks and bumps a night. But after being good for so long, he desired to get obliterated. And he did. Alone in my grandparent's kitchen. Because he could, God damnit! Because he was an adult. Because he worked hard and deserved it. Because he chose to.

The next morning Gumma and Da found their only child passed out on the living room floor in his underwear next to a pee stain on their rug.

They say an alcoholic will have a moments of "incomprehensible demoralization." I don't know about you, but I'd certainly count that as one. I didn't understand why someone would *choose* to do what he did. Why did he make the conscious choice to get so drunk?

The next day, my parents minimized the arguments they had had that led to this second trial separation, and my father returned home. Although, let's be honest, it's hard to convince your parents to let you continue to do what you want after you piss on their furniture.

Chapter 3 — Not So Private Parts

My mother used to call vaginas "ooh who's." She was a very loose blackout drunk, so I think this nickname was derived from her repeatedly slurring, "Ooh, who's in there?" Or perhaps it was her identifying the most important use of her vagina - the "ooh's" she got from sticking things in it. Either way, early on she taught me and Sibby to identify this region of our bodies as dirty and sexual, nothing more.

There is a clinical name for a vagina. It's "vagina." Why not teach us that? No, we had to reiterate her psycho word that her crazy brain made up because it was funny. *Way to humiliate, mom.* The thing is, I didn't realize I was using the incorrect word for it until I got older. I just figured everyone was snickering because I was talking about my private part, not because I was misidentifying it as a lude sex noise. Looking back it must've been funny for a group of day drunks to hear a four year old say, "Mommy, my ooh who itches." But to the four year old who eventually grows up, it was embarrassing to say the least.

When I was very little I became interested in penises. Perhaps my curiosity was piqued by my mother, who would draw pictures of them for me when she was drunk. "They come in different sizes," she told me,

Down the Rabbit Hole

amused by her own visual aids. "Some of them curl up, some are long and skinny, some are short and fat. Some have foreskin, some are veiny. But all are ugly." I do not know what prompted this lecture. Did I ask? Possibly. It's also possible that my lonely mother craved a friend to talk sex with when she was high. Either way, I was curious about dicks.

Occasionally I'd shower with my mother. I'd stand at snatch level staring face to hairy beaver, unable to look anywhere else without getting a face full of soapy water. I'd glance at my mother's vagina, which had dark hair covering it, contrary to the bleach blonde mane on her head, and I felt inferior to her. My vagina was immature, small and bald. Her breasts hung slightly and her nipples were large and hard. My chest was flat with two discolored circles randomly stuck on either side. I wondered when my body would start to look like hers.

I never got to shower with my father. But I wanted to. See, *he* had a body I'd never even seen. I was curious what *his* downstairs looked like. I wanted to see in person what my mother drew drunken caricatures of. I had heard so much about penises, but I'd never seen one in real life. I couldn't wait until I was an adult to see one up close. There was no way I could wait that long! I'd go out of my mind with curiosity.

Down the Rabbit Hole

One day when my father went into the bathroom I felt a rush of bravery. Something told me I could get away with peeking at him while he peed. It could've been that he was in a good mood that day. It could've been that my mother was not home. It could've been a full moon. Nonetheless, I listened to my instincts and cracked the door open to glance. His eyes met mine and I smiled innocently. He glanced down at his penis, then back at me. A wry smile crept across his face, as if to proudly say, *yeah, it's big, isn't it.* My father's penis *was* big, and it seemed somewhat engorged. He held the base of it with one hand, but there was plenty more length extending beyond his grasp. A stream of urine spouted out like a rainbow into a pot of gold. I envied his ability to pee standing up. And so far from the target, yet hitting it perfectly. I felt naughty, but grown up. Like I shared a secret with my daddy. Now I knew what a real, live penis looked like! I couldn't wait until the next time I could spy on him so I could see it again! Now that I knew I was allowed to watch I craved it. I thought about it obsessively. That big protrusive piece of equipment that allowed him to keep his pants up while doing his business! I was so jealous!

I started trying to stand up mid-pee myself, but could never last a whole session without my legs starting to quake and then dribbling. And I was never brave enough to try to pee while standing facing the bowl. I mean, what was I, a sniper?

Down the Rabbit Hole

In the summer my friends and I would swim in our out-of-ground pool, which was an acre away from our house. No one could see us and that gave me courage. I'd be all wet from the water, so I wouldn't care about a few drops of pee getting on my skin. I'd stand in the grass next to the pool, pull my bathing suit to the side, aim and fire. My distance was amazing! The arc I got spanned three feet at least! The privacy, the freedom, I spouted just like my daddy. I loved it. I felt so powerful. So grown up. So dominant.

I'd watch him pee twice more before my mother caught me. She yelled at me, but seemed embarrassed herself. My father defended me. "She's just curious."

"Those are private parts," my mother scolded us. I guess she'd forgotten about her graphic artwork now that it was sober daytime.

Matt and Christopher were two boys I grew up with. Our moms were friends and they lived up the street, so we saw each other regularly. One day when they were over we were playing in the basement rec room, I asked them if I could see their penises. Matt retreated quickly, "no, I can't. But Christopher, you can!" Christopher looked embarrassed, but cornered. His older brother instructing him to do something meant he had to.

Down the Rabbit Hole

"I'll show you *my* private part," I coaxed, sensing his discomfort.

"Christopher, she'll show you hers!" Matt reasoned, knowing he'd reap the benefits of seeing a girl's vag too, but without having to go through the embarrassment of pulling down his pants. Hesitantly, Christopher pulled open his shorts and let his tiny wiener pop out. I was amazed at how small it was. My father's was gigantic compared to his! I guess I'd been expecting them all to be the size of a full grown adult's. It never occurred to me that a six year old's penis would be proportionate to his size. Disappointed, but eager to fulfill my promise, I pulled my shorts and underwear to the side to reveal my vagina to my friends. Christopher barely looked and remained quiet, ashamed to be involved in this activity. Matt was enthralled!

"Woah! Where does the pee come out of?" he asked, leaning in to get a closer look.

"This part," I pulled on my vulva, stretching it out. "There's a pee hole in here." Matt was extremely interested.

"Christopher, look! She's showing us her privates!" but Christopher's interest could not be piqued. Not wanting to seem too easy, I released my

Down the Rabbit Hole

pants, covering my junk again. *Leave 'em wanting more,* I thought. *Maybe next time I can get Matt to show me his. He's older, so his will be bigger...*

Chapter 4 — Return to Sender

I was six years old, my sister just an infant. We were having an overnight visit with my mother at Nana and Papa's, when she realized she could use her parents as free babysitters, and took off for a night of dive bar hopping. Siobhan and I were asleep when our mother drunkenly stumbled home. We awoke to Nana yelling at her that she was too drunk to drive and could not take us with her. I emerged from my room and tentatively peeked around the corner to the ruckus. My mother grabbed me.

"Come on Kate, we're going home," she defiantly slurred. She pulled me out the front door towards her car, which was parked on the street.

"Denise no!" Nana screamed. "I will not let you endanger your children's lives! They are staying here!" But my mother did not listen. She dragged me to the car, threw open the door and shoved me into the backseat.

Commanding the deliverance of her youngest, Denise shouted, "Bring me my baby! You kidnappers! Bring me my child!"

Nana picked me up and took me out of the car, undoing her spawn's mistake before she could make it.

Down the Rabbit Hole

"Denise, you go if you want to, but you are not taking these children in the car with you. You are drunk." I wanted to believe that something got through to her. A hint of humility penetrated the muck of denial. But realistically I think she just wanted to make a dramatic exit. She turned and stormed away, down the road, with no destination in sight. I called after her, but her and her pride kept moving away. It was one of the first times I remember her choosing her disease over us.

The next morning the phone rang. It was my mother calling from a gas station a few towns away. Lord knows how many rides she hitched to get there, but now she was stranded and needed someone to pick her up. So off Papa went to retrieve the hot mess. I ate breakfast silently, dreading her arrival, while Nana gave Sibby her bottle.

"Your mother is very sick, Kate. I want you to know that her disease is not because of you. She's an alcoholic."

"I know," I said. And I did. And even as young as I was, I knew she would probably never choose to get better.

Denise and Papa returned a short while later. Of course, my mother hadn't changed her tune now that she was just hung over instead of in a blackout. She'd had a whole night to rewrite history, proving to herself that her parents were in the wrong and formulating a plan to make sure they were punished. She took Sibby out of Nana's arms and commanded me, again, sans slur, to get in the car. She was livid and we were all to blame.

On the drive back to Middletown my mother informed me that we would never see Nana and Papa again. They were "monsters" who had "tried to take us from her." I remained silent, but inside I was crying. I was powerless over this situation, but yet I was not hopeless. I sensed God holding me, whispering 'everything is going to be OK.'

My mother made up a whole backstory of lies to keep her resentment justified for years. Of course, her childhood had to seem worse than mine and Sibby's. She wanted us to think, *boy, we've really got it good compared to the way our poor mama had it!*

She said that her mother would leave a typewritten note of chores to do when she'd come home from school. The list was so long that no one could ever complete it all in the time given. This gave her parents a justifiable reason to beat her and chain her up in the locked shed in the backyard. The shed was so hot she couldn't breathe, and it had no windows.

Down the Rabbit Hole

She said that her father whipped her. That she was never allowed to have friends. That she was unloved. I don't know if any of this was true at all, but according to Nana it was all a fabricated story made up by a sick mind.

My mother said that Papa never told her he loved her. Now, if you knew Papa you'd believe that one was true. Not because he was unloving, but because he was so old fashioned he seemed to believe that nurturing was the mother's role and he didn't feel comfortable participating in it. Papa liked to work, eat, watch TV and listen to his CB radio. That was it. He didn't like to travel. He didn't even like to leave the house. He was just simple.

Nana volunteered at a local shelter, where she obtained most of her wardrobe, food, and gifts for me and my sister. I often wondered if the things she took from the Cornerstone were meant for people much less fortunate, but I didn't want to upset Nana so I never brought it up. I think she thought she was entitled to first dibs on donations because it was payment for her volunteer work. *Kinda negates the definition of 'volunteer'... but what did I know?*

Down the Rabbit Hole

For eight years we weren't allowed to see Nana and Papa… but we did see them. Nana contacted Gumma and Da and alerted them to this whole dysfunctional mess, and they would secretly bring me and Sibby to Abdow's in Rocky Hill every few months to meet up with Nana and Papa for lunch. They sent birthday and Christmas cards to Gumma and Da's house, and sometimes we'd call them from their house too. It was a secret I cherished between my grandparents and me, as well as a secret "fuck you" to my no-good mother.

Nana kept scrapbooks for me throughout the years. In one, I found the following letter. It had been opened, but "Return to Sender" was written on the envelope in Denise's handwriting.

8-18-85

Dear Denise:

Dad and I are returning the check you wrote us because we feel you cannot afford it and we do not need it. You were in no condition to know how much you had spent on the weekend and I am sure you need the money for more important things.

Down the Rabbit Hole

I think you should know that you were so drunk that you jeopardized both children's lives by putting them in your car and attempting to drive when you could not even see. You asked me to clean your glasses when it was your eyes that were foggy. You told Kate that if she got out of the car you would MURDER her.

I think you should seek help and be very careful of how you handle the children because Kate is so sensitive that she could have very serious emotional problems if things go on this way. She is only 6 and not responsible for the care of her sister.

Screaming only makes the situation worse. Kate and Siobhan are both babies in a sense and "minor infractions" are to be expected.

I hope you will be careful in the future not to repeat the scene you made here at any other place. The neighbors sure got an earful.

Love to you all,
Mom

Chapter 5 — The Big Black Babysitter

Not surprisingly, my parents were bigots. I mean sure, they had a few acquaintances who fell into the "minority" category, but that didn't stop them from making racist jokes whenever possible. My father referred to the back of theatre balconies as "nigger heaven," our Italian neighbors were "guineas", Puerto Ricans were "Spics." If an opportunity presented itself to make an ethnically derogatory joke, my parents jumped at it. Shitting on other people was one of the few things that made them both laugh.

One of their attempts at humor came in the form of a threat. When I was five years old my parents warned me that if I was bad they were going to get the Big, Black Babysitter to come. She was a morbidly obese, mean double-dipper who'd slap me into shape if I got out of line. I was a pretty good kid; they scared me enough that I'd learned to just behave, so this ongoing joke was more for their own amusement. "Eat all your dinner, Punkie, or the Big Black Babysitter's going to come make you eat it," my father would say at the dinner table, attempting to illicit a snicker from my mother.

Down the Rabbit Hole

My father was a stagehand: carpentry and automation. He worked on national tours of musicals, so a few months later we moved to San Francisco with the cast and crew of his latest show, *42nd Street.* One Monday night my parents wanted to go out to dinner so they called a local babysitting agency to come watch me and my sister. This was pre-internet so you couldn't go online and racially pre-screen candidates yourself. You just had to trust that this agency had done their homework and would send someone "appropriate." My parents were given verbal confirmation from the receptionist that a qualified sitter would be there at seven PM.

An hour later, guess who came to dinner? Sorry. Just kidding. An hour later the doorbell rang. I followed my father as he went to answer it. I was excited for a babysitter. They were never drunk, and always let me do whatever I wanted. I got to eat *three* popsicles if I wanted, and stay up watching TV until late at night! It was freedom from the tired, drunken routine I had come to know so well.

When my father opened the door I was bubbling with anticipation... until he revealed who stood on the other side: an overweight, 60-ish, dark-skinned black woman. Immediately my thoughts raced. *This has been a trap! My parents weren't going out to dinner! They'd hired this woman to beat me to death! And they're all just standing there smiling! They were*

Down the Rabbit Hole

going to enjoy it! I burst into tears, "it's the Big, Black Babysitter!" I wailed. My parent's faces turned to horror.

"No, no! No, no, Kate, uhh..." My mother searched for an acceptable justification as she swooped me up and into the other room. My father laughed a condescending chortle which let me know I'd be getting it later. The babysitter stood on the stoop, her eyebrows raised as she awaited an explanation.

"Sorry about that. She watches too much TV. How ya doin'?" My father stepped aside and welcomed her in with an extended arm. Skeptical and unsatisfied, she came inside. My mother shut the bedroom door and crouched down to me.

"What the hell is wrong with you!?" she yelled in a whisper.

"You called the Big Black Babysitter! What did I do?" I pleaded in terror.

"Nothing! Jesus Christ, that was a joke, Kate! You *never* repeat what we joke about!" I began to calm down.

"So, I'm not in trouble?" I confirmed.

Down the Rabbit Hole

"You are now," she clarified.

Down the Rabbit Hole

Chapter 6 — The Life I Wanted vs. The Life I Had

My mother had a knack for finding cheap apartments in dangerous neighborhoods. In 1984 my dad's show took us to San Francisco and my mother signed the month-to-month lease on a one-bedroom in the "Tenderloin," San Fransisco's ghetto. Our building was attached to another building and my sister and I had a hobby of throwing my mother's hairbrush out of the window onto the roof of the neighboring building. My parents had to go downstairs, climb out of our Chinese acrobat downstairs neighbor's window onto the neighboring roof, and retrieve the flying hairbrush more than once. It was funny to see our parents on the roof. I wished they would've jumped off it.

I had to be enrolled in a huge, inner city kindergarten in San Francisco so that I didn't get held back my first year of school. This school was bigger and way different from my tiny school in Middletown. As a white girl I was part of the minority in this school. The "playground" was a large blacktop with two basketball hoops and graffitied walls that you could stand on top of if you were brave and rebellious enough to climb up there. It seemed the students spent an inordinate amount of time out here before "school" actually began. Looking back I wonder if the teachers were just unable to get their shit together to start class on time. Anyway, I was terrified of being on the playground with all these black people! My parents only said bad things about them, like how they were thieves, rapists and murderers, so naturally I was scared of them.

No one ever bullied me at this school, though. No one bothered me at all, actually.

As I was walking up the stairs one day a black girl from my class ran up to me. "Hi Kathy," she said.

"It's Kate," I answered.

"No, your name is Kathy," she replied.

"Ok," I accepted and began to adapt to my new name.

My kindergarten was far away from our apartment. My dad had to take me on two different city busses every morning to get there. We'd leave forty five minutes before school started to get there on time.

One day while waiting for the second bus with my dad an old bum approached me. "Hiiiiiii," he marveled, "how are you?" He took my hand and kissed it.

Down the Rabbit Hole

"Here, here, get away," my father protectively shooed him.

"She's beautiful!" the bum complemented my father on his work.

"Thank you, now go away," my dad replied. I was so flattered! I wanted to say, "no, let him stay! Tell me more, kind sir!" But he respectfully left, his eyes glued to me wide with wonder as he departed.

"Daddy, he said I was beautiful!" I excitedly repeated to my protector.

"You are beautiful, Punkie. Wash your hands as soon as you get to school."

I made a friend during my brief life in San Fran. Her name was Jennifer and *she* was a beautiful, rich white girl with long, thick blonde hair that looked like it was professionally done every day. She went to a private school and I met her at the park with her nanny one day. I don't know what her parents did for a living, as I only met them once briefly, but she was always with that nanny. She lived in a huge, gorgeous co op that looked like a fairy tale castle. "Let's draw in the yellow room," she said one day, then opened the double doors to reveal a high ceilinged living room-type space furnished all in yellow and white.

Down the Rabbit Hole

I literally exclaimed, "wow!" as she showed me inside.

"I know," she agreed very down-to-earth-ly. For a girl with such wealth Jennifer was very non-pretentious. She did not show off or brag, and she agreed that her home was impressive, almost embarrassingly so. The curtains alone in this room must've cost more than my father made in a year, and I wouldn't dare sit on the Baroque style furniture. We laid our drawing paper on the rug and drew. I tried to capture on paper my magical surroundings, but I was not that artistically gifted.

The next time I visited Jennifer's she showed me the purple room. Again, as expected by its title, this living-room type space was furnished all in dark purples and oak. The window wear was thick and heavy, blocking the light so as to enhance the theme. I didn't like this room as much as the yellow room. It reminded me too much of the dark drug den that was my home. I liked light and sun. I liked happy and bright. I suggested we go to another room.

Jennifer was an only child, so she was happy to have a friend. Her nanny seemed glad she'd met me as well. She welcomed me every day with a smile and encouraged my visits. Jennifer had a great imagination. She was really an ideal child; very fun and kind. She shared her things and

Down the Rabbit Hole

never said a negative word about anything. I never met any of her other friends, so I don't know if she had any or not. But she didn't seem lonely or sad. Just normal and well-adjusted, which was foreign and impressive to me. I wished I had a life like hers.

One day she suggested we have a scavenger hunt. She collected some things from her room and employed her nanny to hide them. "We need prizes," she said, so off to the uptown pharmacy the three of us went to buy ourselves prizes for finding Jennifer's own toys in her own house. I already loved this game! Apparently there were going to be no losers! Jennifer was very good at buying prizes. Without hesitation she gathered a basket of candies, stickers, buttons and small toys for which to reward ourselves. She even remembered to buy little gift packs to wrap them all in. She very fairly thought to buy two of everything, equal in value but differing in color. I was humbled by the quality of the prizes she so casually purchased. Well, her nanny paid with her parent's money, to be fair, but still, I couldn't believe how generous she was allowed to be!

When we got back to her house she wrapped the trinkets in their gift bags and let me pick which one I wanted. First things first - prizes. Then we got to hunting... which was over rather quickly, as we were excellent scavengers and her home was too clean to really hide anything for long. The prize-assembling portion of the day had easily taken three times as

Down the Rabbit Hole

long as the actual hunt. But I had had a blast! What a fun day that was! So innocent, so child-like.

The next day my dad made me a piñata. He put some small toys in a paper bag and hung it on a rope off a small hook in the ceiling. "Don't swing on the rope," he reprimanded harshly as I immediately tried to swing on the rope. He blindfolded me, then handed me a spatula. My mother and he laughed as I repeatedly swung and missed by long shots. They took pictures and we bonded like a normal family for 15 minutes or so.

They then retired to their bedroom. It was the middle of the day, so I assumed they were taking a nap. I wasn't tired, so I swung on the paper bag until it broke free from the ceiling, taking the hook and a small piece of plaster with it. Afraid, I laid down by the wall waiting for my parents to awake and beat me. Then I heard it. My parent's bed squeaking rhythmically and my mother's phlegmy moaning. *Oh, gross!* I knew what was going on. I listened, picturing what was taking place on the other side of the wall, and it drew me deep into an angry, sad, disgusted place - the rabbit hole. The tunnel of negative thoughts, self pity and fear. Too scared to make any noise that might interrupt them, I laid still, remained quiet and listened. Because I had nowhere to go, I heard it all.

Down the Rabbit Hole

A little while later my father emerged from the bedroom. "I told you not to fucking swing on the rope!" he screamed, as he saw the homemade piñata still attached to the rope, but not to the ceiling. He grabbed me by the arm and pulled me off the ground. He smacked me hard on the butt, then pushed me back down to the floor. He yelled at me, pointing a finger too close to my face. "That's the last time we ever do something nice for you!"

He stomped away, into the bedroom, and slammed the door. I sat there in a heap on the dirty floor, alone, imagining what my friend Jennifer was doing at that very moment. Further and further down the rabbit hole I fell…

Chapter 7 — Kids? What Kids?

My parents were not willing to change their lives at all now that they had kids. That sometimes meant acting like we weren't even there. I remember one time when I was around seven or so, I was watching TV in the living room by myself. My father came in and, very deliberately, sat down in the chair and changed the channel. No, "Hi Punkie, I wanna watch football. Do you mind if I change the channel?" No, "Hi honey, do you wanna watch football with Daddy?" No, "fuck off, it's my TV and I'm changing the channel." Nothing. Just silence, which was more hurtful than words. A non acknowledgement. A you-don't-exist, you're-irrelevant. And that's how I felt...

Yes, he saw me. He knew it was *me* sitting there watching *Sesame Street*. But he was intentionally, silently belittling me. Letting me know that he was the adult, so common courtesy didn't apply. He didn't *have* to say anything to me. He was the master of the house because he paid for it. I had to respect him, but he didn't have to respect me.

I sat for a moment feeling very small, helpless, alone, and invisible. So, if that was his goal, he accomplished it. I even gave him a few beats, thinking maybe he'd say something to me. Invite me to stay? Just smile and say hi? I was frozen into a state of lonely silence, too scared to speak up and say something first. I was afraid he'd yell at me or that I'd just start to cry. He did not speak, so I left. I went into my room and fell deeper and deeper into the rabbit hole.

He often did things like this, and I wonder if he ever felt bad at all? When I left the room did he feel a pang of regret? Did he think about calling out to me and inviting me to stay? ... Or was he glad I left? Was his goal to estrange me? To make me feel unwelcome in my own home?

Well, if my parents wanted me to feel estranged they accomplished that many times over. Never so much so as when I watched them doing it, though. That takes the cake.

I *heard* my parents have sex many times. We lived in a small two-bedroom house until I was ten years old and they'd leave both bedroom doors ajar at night. My mother was very vocal during sex, so I'd hear her moaning along with the consistent, thumping waves of the waterbed. I wanted to scream, "I can hear you, you fucking perverts! Your children are twenty fucking feet from you!" But obviously I did not.

I *saw* them have sex twice, the first of which was when I was ten years old. We were living in a one-bedroom apartment in Chicago. All four of us

Down the Rabbit Hole

slept in the one bedroom. My parents in the bed, my sister on a fold out armchair and me on the fold out sleeper chair on the floor. One night they thought we were asleep. Well, I *had been,* anyway. My "bed" was at the end of their bed against the wall, leaving a small walkway between my bed and theirs, so I had a perfect view of the fornication that would forever scar my brain. I was awoken by the noises. My father bouncing awkwardly from left to right on top of my mother. Her vagina must've been cavernous because from the way he was moving it seemed he couldn't get to all of it at once. Thank God they were under the covers! I'm sure I would've wound up in a psych ward never to speak again if I had seen details. My mother was moaning, "Oh Eddie! Hump me!" My father stayed silent, although his athletics left him panting. He seemed to be on some sort of mission. Like he was running for his life or something. This session lasted way too long. At least five minutes. My mother remained in her lazy bottom position, while my father did all the work, just like in real life. When it was over there were no orgasmic sounds, thank God or I might've gone deaf right then. It just finally ended anti-climactically. I shut my eyes as my father emerged from the bed. If they knew I was awake I would be in big trouble for spying on them. I squeezed my eyes shut, trying to erase the image as if my brain were an etch-a-sketch.

Down the Rabbit Hole

The second time I saw them do it was in Oak Park, Illinois days before my mother would have my father arrested and he would leave her. We were living in a one-room hotel room until our sublet became available. Too cheap to spring for two rooms my parents boned like Sibby and I *weren't* in the adjacent bed attempting to sleep. I might've been drifting off, but after their escapade began I laid frozen the rest of the night. Again, my father plowed into my mother as if he were trying to make his wrestling weight. It was embarrassing to witness. If you were ever casting an awkward porn, these two would be perfect. God, their sex made me mad! And their kissing! That enraged me. It was so loud I could hear it in the next room. Slurp, slop, smack. Ewww! What the fuck are you kissing for anyway? You hate each other! I was so happy a few days later when my father filed for divorce, for I'd never have to see their disgusting sex again.

Down the Rabbit Hole

Chapter 8 — Dunkin' Donuts

One day when I was around five years old my very put-upon parents dragged me with them to run some errands. They hated errands. Firstly, because errands meant spending money. Money that could be used for cocaine and vodka. Money they -- well, my father -- worked hard for, and was already taxed on. The idea of having to pay sales tax on top of that for daily necessities was enough to make him set fire to the Constitution! Secondly, running errands meant they were not sleeping. I knew by this time that, for my parents, to be awake was to be angry. Doing anything besides drugs and drinking was a major inconvenience. They'd be angry all day until they got their relief at night. Lastly, they hated having me with them. I slowed them down. I cannot tell you how often I heard, "Come ON! Let's GO!" as I ran to keep up with their long legged strides.

The first stop on this typical, depressing day was Dunkin' Donuts for something to quickly stuff in our faces. The three of us sat down at the counter and the cashier approached us and asked, "coffee?" I call her a cashier, not a waitress, because it was a Dunkin' Donuts. Not exactly a place that requires waitstaff. Nor is it a place where anyone could make a living on tips. So this poor woman who was making minimum wage stocking, cleaning and ringing up patrons at the ass crack of dawn also

Down the Rabbit Hole

had the additional unpleasant duty of waiting on impatient, most likely non-tipping assholes who were too cheap to go out to a real, sit-down breakfast.

My father gave her a dirty look, "yeah," he said condescendingly. I could tell the nice lady had done something to piss him off already, though I had no idea what. Not that it was out of the ordinary for someone to set my father off with just one word. Hell, a sideways glance had been known to enrage him. She returned promptly with two cups of coffee. My parents remained silent; my father testing her waitressing capabilities, my mother staring into space, likely fantasizing about her next drink containing alcohol.

"Do you want something to drink for her?" the cashier asked, regarding me. *There ya go!*, I silently applauded, *surely that was what Dad was looking for to pass his acceptable level of service test.*

"Orange juice," my father curtly replied. She left again to retrieve my beverage and returned with an OJ and the check. Wrong move, lady. "Jesus fucking Christ! Can't we order what we want!?!" My father exploded. I could read his thoughts. *Why didn't she ask us if we wanted anything to eat?! Couldn't she read our minds?! It's **her** job to ask us if we're hungry, not **our** job to tell her! Initiating communication is a very clear job*

Down the Rabbit Hole

requirement at Dunkin' Donuts! Doesn't she know fucking anything?! My mom finally snapped to. The woman looked embarrassed and annoyed. She glanced around to see who was looking at this scene. Everyone was. A man who sat at a nearby table reading the paper, a woman and her baby at a table across the way, and another employee who crept around the coffee machine to peek at the scene. I looked down with my own shame and embarrassment as my father continued. He stood up, took out his wallet and threw some money on the counter. "Let's go!" he commanded. I could tell Denise was embarrassed by this outburst, and knew she had no idea what had caused it. The two of us dutifully obliged my father and ran-walked to follow him to the car. So... no chocolate honey glazed donut for me, then? Guess not. That was sad.

My father took opening his car door as another opportunity to express his rage at the horrific service he'd just received in this five-star rated donut shop. He threw the driver's side door open and then slammed it shut, as if that'd show those assholes who they dared give subpar service to! I hated that I had to get in that car. And without the comfort and solace of my best friend donut too. Today was not looking up. My dad peeled out of the parking lot, cutting someone off and giving my mother and me heart attacks in the process. Whelp, now he had someone to blame today's bad mood on. Great. And so early in the day, too. Sigh. I'd stay extra quiet today and go right to my room when we got home. Maybe I could go to Gumma and Da's tonight. That would be *my* relief.

I told Gumma about this incident a few weeks after it happened. She had trouble accepting that my father was capable of doing anything wrong, but when I told her how he'd lost his temper at an unassuming victim, she replied with disapproval. "Oohh, he should not have done that," she scolded, "She was just trying to do her job. He was in the wrong…"

"I know," I replied. And I did.

Down the Rabbit Hole

Chapter 9 — The Common Crash

One typical morning, while I was watching my little sister so my mother could nap off a hangover, Sibby wouldn't stop crying. I don't know why. I was only 6 and she was a baby. Maybe she was hungry, maybe she had an earache, maybe she was suddenly aware of the horrible home life she'd been born into and screaming for salvation. Either way, she woke my mother up. Denise bombarded from her room and screamed, "you keep that baby quiet!" She grabbed a knife from the knife rack, "you shut her up or I'll kill you both! I'll slaughter you to pieces!"

I held my sister tight against me as we both cried, Sibby an infant's sobs, me a scared child's whimper. "Ok, ok, I'm sorry," I begged. "I'll keep her quiet. I'm sorry."

Denise angrily and deliberately stomped back into her room and slammed and locked her door. I felt relief, yet also panic. I had to make this baby stay quiet until mommy got the sleep she needed to calm her coke-addled nerves. I begged Sibby to stay quiet with coos and shushes, but when she started to cry again I held my hand over her mouth and silently cried with her. Just an hour or two more until that eye opening shut eye would make Denise feel the inevitable remorse for threatening her kid's lives to get an afternoon snooze. Just a few more hours until that monster turned back into a human being.

Down the Rabbit Hole

Chapter 10 — Sick Brains

When I was six years old I got the flu. I had a fever and was sweating, and also had the chills. I was nauseous and weak. There's not much you can do for the flu except rest, drink water and wait. Well my mother, being the impatient person that she was, felt inconvenienced by the ill-timing of my sickness.

She invited me to sleep in her room because I was sweating and she had an air conditioner. But also, my dad was on the road with a show and she hated being alone. I was so sick. I didn't have the energy to provide the emotional support she needed from me that night. I laid in my parent's waterbed while my mother sat up smoking Barclays and drinking vodka/tonics beside me, pretending to play the role of caring mother. The waves of the bed gave me motion sickness. The second hand smoke upset my stomach. I tried to hold it in as long as I could, but eventually I couldn't. I threw up on the comforter.

"Son of a bitch!!" she exclaimed, her arms flying above her head in disgust. She jumped off the bed, grabbed the back of my neck and flung me into the bathroom over the toilet. Her hands gripped my head, as if to say, *this is where you're supposed to puke, you dipshit!* I tried to obey,

Down the Rabbit Hole

but I was done vomiting for the time being. I think that angered her more because she continued to yell. "You stupid fucking child! All over my bed!" I stared down the inside of the toilet, where it was safer. My inner God voice soothed me, *It's all going to be ok.*

"I'm sorry," I sincerely apologized, and weakly stood up. My mother flushed the toilet in a huff, although I'd only spat out a little bile.

"Wash your mouth out," she instructed.

I hobbled back to her bed. I don't know why. Maybe because the A/C felt good. Maybe I was afraid she'd yell at me if I tried to slink into my own room. I wasn't strong enough to climb to the top bunk of my own bed, anyway. I had sick brain. Denise folded up her blanket to remove it from the bed. I stumbled back onto the sheets-only waterbed, trembling.

"Look at this!" she screamed. "Look at what you did!" I turned over just enough to see that she was holding up her comforter, my vomit splattered in the middle. "You stupid piece of shit!" I was just too powerless to do anything but close my eyes. I fell asleep.

I don't know how much time passed. An hour? Maybe two? I woke up to my mother crying. The overhead light had been turned off, but the bedside light on my side of the bed was on. My mother sobbed, "I'm so sorry, honey. I'm so sorry I got mad at you." I suddenly felt a little better.

"It's ok," I comforted softly.

"No, no it's not ok. You're sick. I shouldn't have yelled at you. You didn't mean to throw up on the bed." She hugged me and I felt healed, whole. Like the God voice had promised. He worked quickly this time. Everything was ok.

Down the Rabbit Hole

Chapter 11 — Step 1?

I was six years old. It was December in Connecticut. Snow was on the ground and the sun reflected harshly off the ice, which covered everything. My parents were hungover from a heavy night of drinking and doing blow, so my mother went to take a nap while my father was to drive me to Gumma and Da's house.

I was so happy to be going there. My house caused headaches, stress-related the doctors would later diagnose. Gumma and Da's house was a safe haven. There, they kept the curtains open, inviting the sun in to help boost the temperature and the mood. At my house the shades were always drawn, because sunlight reminded Ed and Denise that it was the day they were sleeping away. Gumma and Da's was a brightly lit oasis of warmth, whereas my parents' house was cold, dark and dingy. You never knew what time it was inside my home. At Gumma and Da's you could tell the time by the shadows cast from the sun pouring through the many windows.

My father was not well this day. It was early, but he had not slept and appeared to be out of it. We got in the car and he began to unload on me.

Down the Rabbit Hole

"Your mother thinks I'm having an affair with Nancy."

I did not know who Nancy was and I was startled into silence by this confession. What could I say? I couldn't ask him if he was, for fear of that sounding like an accusation. I didn't want to seem like I was taking sides with my mother. I didn't want him to think we were in cahoots against him. So I stayed silent.
"I'm not," he answered my thoughts. "I told her that, but she doesn't believe me."

Again, I said nothing. But at that moment I felt close to my father. He was trusting me with this revelation. Perhaps he wanted me to take sides with him. To be his comrade in his fight to win my mother's trust. I felt honored to hear this adult information. For the first time in my relationship with him I felt like an equal.

He seemed deep in thought. He sat, staring at the steering wheel. So I sat and waited for him to continue. I was invested now. Eager to develop this new bond, to collaborate, to solve. I kept my gaze fixed on the radio, as if his eye space was private and necessary for his contemplation… then he started to snore. When I looked up, he was asleep, with his mouth slightly agape. Behind the wheel of the car, keys in the ignition, his six year old daughter buckled in beside him, passed out at one o'clock in the afternoon in our driveway.

Perhaps this is what the first step in AA is alluding to when they ask you to describe how your life has become unmanageable. *Wait a minute - how dare you!? He has a good paying job! So what if he just wanted to take a little nappy poo in his car!? He pays taxes for this driveway, so fuck you!* I sat for a few moments thinking he might wake up feeling refreshed and take me on my merry way to Bend Lane, but he did not stir. It became apparent that this was last night's sleep he was having here, not a brief cat nap to recharge his engine.

So I got out of the car and went inside. My mother and sister were both asleep. I quietly dialed Gumma and Da's phone number. Da answered. "Can you come get me? My dad fell asleep in the car."

The silent beat that followed was audible. I could hear Da's thoughts. *You've got to be kidding me. Have you been drinking, Eddie? You've got to get it together. You're a father now. You must stop this!* But, "ok, I'll be there soon," was all he said.

I went to the living room to watch out the window for Da. I heard my father come in through the kitchen door. I was scared that he would yell at me for leaving the car while he was talking to me. That he would threaten to kill me if I told my mother that he'd confided in me. That he'd make me get back in the car and angrily drunk drive me to Gumma and Da's, getting into an accident and killing us on the way. But he just stumbled down the hallway and into his bedroom. Not even stopping to see if I was ok. I don't think he even knew I was there. He probably had no recollection of how he got to the car, let alone why he had been in it. I breathed a sigh of relief as he shut and locked the bedroom door.

I waited and waited for Da to arrive. Perhaps he explained to Gumma why he had to come get me instead of my father dropping me off. Perhaps that sparked a longer conversation about my parents' larger issue which, even though they didn't want to acknowledge it publicly, was too big to ignore altogether... Or maybe he just couldn't find his car keys. Either way the five minute drive took him forty-five minutes. I jumped up as the large, white Oldsmobile approached and went outside to hop right in.

I was relieved. I would make it to Gumma and Da's today, and the rest of the day would be ok! Good, even! I was sure I could use this situation to convince them to let me sleep over tonight! Yay! Everything was going to be ok.

Down the Rabbit Hole

Chapter 12 — My Safe Haven

My Gumma and Da's house was a place of safety. It felt warm there. And not just because my grandmother always had the thermostat on eighty degrees. I felt warm inside too. Like you're supposed to feel in your home: safe, secure, happy, loved.

Gumma and Da slept in separate bedrooms. Gumma had the master bedroom and Da had my dad's childhood room. I'd sleep in Gumma's room with her in the big bed when I'd sleep over. Nana and Papa had separate bedrooms too, so I thought it was normal to sleep far away from your spouse while still remaining in the same house. Gumma and Nana explained that Da and Papa snored so that's why the separate rooms. I bought that.

Gumma had a sparing, but hilarious, dry sense of humor. When I was very little I used to sit on her lap and she'd bounce me up and down while she hummed "Call to Post." With perfect comic timing she'd open her knees so I'd fall through them, then pull me right back up without missing a beat, as if I were a clumsy, but determined jockey, or a drunk marionette. I'd giggle hysterically every time.

Down the Rabbit Hole

At night Gumma would make me a bubble bath. She used dish soap because she said it made better bubbles than bubble bath, and she sat next to the faucet swishing the water and soap around to create a mountain of suds for me to climb into. I had a tub full of bath toys: Barbies, my little ponies, Rub-a-dub dog. I'd stay in there until the water got cold and my fingers and toes pruned. Forty five minutes to an hour baths were the norm. Sometimes Gumma would even heat up water on the stove then bring it upstairs to heat up the bath for me so I could stay in longer.

I loved imagining in there. I'd pretend I was Barbie, living in a California mansion with a cute boyfriend and a red convertible. That was the life I wanted when I got older. I wanted long blonde hair, like I already had, and a rockin' bikini body, which I didn't. I wanted to have achieved my dreams of moving to Hollywood and becoming an actress. I wanted to be living in a beach house that I'd bought with my own hard earned money. I wanted to prove to my doubting parents that I could be someone. That I could achieve goals despite their best attempts to beat me down. To hold me back. To make me believe I couldn't. I could do more than just dream. I could overcome.

I'd imagine I was a My Little Pony. Sprinkles - the light purple pegasus with the blue hair and duck tattoos - that one was my favorite. She was the level-headed pony. Majesty, the white unicorn with the blue flower symbols was the bitch. We loved her, but everyone silently judged her and favored me. I was the leader because I was so reasonable, approachable and kind. I was the trusted friend. Other ponies came to me for advice, and they were so grateful for my calm wisdom. I was a reliable mane to cry on. I'd empathize, and then make them feel better. I could talk any pony off a ledge.

When it was time for bed at Gumma's house, we'd climb up the stairs together slowly while she sang, *"Pardon me boys, is that the Chattanooga choo choo? On track twenty nine…"* I'd slowly crawl on my hands and knees a few steps ahead of Gumma, and she'd playfully pull me by the leg so I'd slide down a few steps to meet her, as if she were trying to win a race by thwarting her opponent. Again, never missing a note. She always made me laugh.

Once in her bedroom we'd get on our knees and pray. The Lord's Prayer. "Our father who art in heaven. Hallow'd be thy name. Thy kingdom come. Thy will be done. On earth as it is in heaven. Give us this day our daily bread and forgive us our trespasses as we forgive those who've trespassed against us. Lead us not into temptation. But deliver us from evil. Amen."

Down the Rabbit Hole

Then she'd tuck me in. She'd make a nest of pillows around me as if I were a baby bird. A pillow on each side of me and two under head. Safely surrounded by comfort. She'd give me a baby bottle of chocolate milk. Until I was about ten (yes, ten) and my parents said I was too old for a bottle. Then she'd sing me a lullaby. "Turah lurah lurah. Turah lurah lye. Turah lurah lurah. Hush now don't you cry. Turah lurah lurah. Turah lurah lye. Turah lurah lurah. That's an Irish lullaby." She'd continue to sing as she left the room and descended the stairs. She wouldn't stop until she was entirely out of earshot. As if to say, *I'm with you even if we're apart.* As if to reassure me that I was safe and she was always nearby. By the time she'd come up to bed I'd be sound asleep.

I loved my nighttime rituals at Gumma and Da's house. They were homey. Loving. Routine. Not like the unpredictable chaos at my house. I never knew what was gonna happen at night there, but I knew it was likely to be bad. I was never scared at Gumma and Da's. I was safe there. Secure, content and loved.

Down the Rabbit Hole

Chapter 13 — Myself / My Friend

I always wished I had a twin. I wanted someone who was going through the same chaos to talk to. So when I was five I started pretending I *was* a twin. Our names were Katrina and Katerina. We were Italian. Katerina was pronounced with an Italian accent.

The invention of the twins was one of the first times I remember escaping into my own head. Solving problems by using my imagination. Relying on myself to make me feel better. I'd pretend I was both twins and we'd have entire conversations. We got along so well! We were perfect sisters. We had each other's backs. One lifted the other up when she was sad. Encouraged the other. Supported the other's dreams of singing. We never fought. We shared clothes. We were the best of friends.

Katrina and Katerina weren't "imaginary friends." They were parts of me. A part of myself that was lonely comforted by a part of myself that was good at comforting. A part of myself who saw the good in a bad situation, talking up the part of myself that was sad. In a way, my imaginary twin was also the mother I wished I'd had. My Gumma's nurturing nature in a peer's imaginary body.

Down the Rabbit Hole

Katrina and Katerina were singers. For Christmas one year Gumma and Da bought me a microphone and little speakers. They set it up on a large table in the basement: my stage. This is where Katrina and Katerina would rehearse. They were child stars. They were only nine years old, but had made enough money to support themselves for years so they didn't have to rely on their evil parents. They toured the country by tour bus performing concerts. Their tour manager took care of the administrative stuff, like hiring tutors, etc. The other stuff they handled on their own. These girls were smart and level headed. When their tour was over they had a TV show about their life on Nickelodeon. They were never bored. Never without work. And, because they each had each other, they were never alone.

In my fantasy world the twins' parents wished they'd treated them better and were remorseful about abusing them. But Katrina and Katerina had become successful, self-sufficient pre-adolescents as a result of it, so they weren't bitter. They were grateful for their turbulent past. It gave them creative motivation.

I pretended I was Katrina most of the time, because she had the prettier name. She was the younger twin. The one who needed a little more encouragement. She relied on her slightly older sister a little more than Katerina relied on her. Katerina was a smidgen more of a mother figure. I guess part of me really wanted that dynamic. The little girl in me sought a reliable mom. In this world, I had that.

As I got older, Katrina and Katerina dissipated, but I held on to their purpose. I continued to lift myself up out of sad places. I continued to delve into parts of myself where hope lived and I found that hope grew. There was rarely a scenario that I couldn't learn from. Almost never a time when I couldn't see that there'd be a rainbow after the storm. I believe in faith because I had it. There was no evidence that my life would get better eventually. Only a voice somewhere inside me that assured me it would. Call it God, or my imaginary alter ego. Call it crazy or call it hope. I'm thankful for it. It allowed me to live happier even when there wasn't anything to be happy about.

Chapter 14 — Drunken Abuse and Sober Promises

I was seven years old. Sibby was two. We were asleep in our room in our tiny two bedroom house on Bixby street when I was awoken by what sounded like a heavy body falling to the ground, and a chair hitting the wall. My eyes shot open as my dad accidentally nudged our bedroom door open as he dragged my mother down the hall by her hair. She was on the ground, her hands grasping on to his, locked on her head. They were both obviously obliterated. I sat up in my top bunk, horrified at the scene unfolding in front of me. My mother caught my eye and screamed for help.

"Kate! Call 911! Help me!" But I was frozen. I could not move for fear of my father turning his rage on me. I didn't want him to think I was taking her side.

I bet she started in on him, I thought. She suspected he was having an affair with one of the women on his show. I'll bet she began her accusations once he got home from work. And by that time, she was already completely in the bag. Her tongue was loose and ready to flap insults. All he wanted was some peace and quiet. He deserved a subservient little wife since he brought home all the bacon. But my mother was rebellious and would not sit idly by and be disrespected. And since her fears assured her of such, she was convinced my father was cheating.

My mother knew how to push my father's buttons in order to get her beating. She knew how to rile him up so he'd hit her. And that's what she wanted. Then she had the bruises to prove that she was a battered martyr. Battered women get special treatment. Judges grant abused wives more spousal support. Employers dote on poor female employees who work just to get a break from their abusive husbands. Friends and family give abused women who drink a break, because they understand that they're only drinking to ease the pain inflicted by their husbands. Twenty-six years old and this was my mother's sick, manipulative game.

My father did not let go of my mother when he learned I was awake and watching. His ego trumped any awareness that he was traumatizing his young children by subjecting them to this scene. But he did flail around and slam our bedroom door shut, keeping hold of Denise's messy mane with one hand. As if it wasn't too late to shield us from what I'd already seen. As if to say to my mother, "fuck you, bitch! This is between you and me!" As if the paper-thin door would stifle her terrorizing screams. It might have been a pointless gesture, because the damage was already done, but in that moment it was the most fatherly thing he was capable of doing. Trying to shield us from further harm.

Down the Rabbit Hole

He must've let her go after that, because the ruckus stopped. She must've called 911 herself, because soon I heard the faint sounds of sirens in the distance becoming louder and louder until they arrived at our house. I heard the pounding on the door and I heard my mother answer it, and again I heard her crying. I shook with fear in my bed as my mind drew pictures of what was happening on the other side of my closed door. I heard a police scanner, a stretcher being unfolded, and I heard everyone leave. Then I heard nothing and I wondered if my sister and I were alone in the house.

Eventually I was able to fall asleep. The following morning my father was gentler with Sibby and me as we visited my mother in the hospital. Apparently he, not the alcohol or drugs, had damaged one of her kidneys and she'd been admitted to the hospital overnight.

The three of us walked into my mother's room and gave her hugs. She hugged us hard and told us she loved us so much, "more than anything in the world." It was her guilt talking. These words always followed a night of incomprehensible demoralization. I'd learned to take them with a grain of salt. They didn't mean anything.

Down the Rabbit Hole

I was told to take my sister out into the hall while mommy and daddy talked. They shut the door. We sat and waited a long time. I can only assume they were in there making well-intentioned plans to cut down on their drinking, to communicate better, to be better spouses. My father probably swore he wasn't having an affair and to never hit her again. My mother most likely promised to talk to him instead of throwing crazy accusations around and to not get shit-faced until *after* he got home at night. When my father finally emerged from the hospital room he seemed lighter, happier, hopeful. He played Good Daddy that whole day, taking us to McDonalds and the local video store. But only until my mother came home from the hospital and that whole we-can-make-it-work attitude proved impossible to practice. What is it they say? The road to hell is paved with good intentions.

Chapter 15 — Bullied

My parents used to buy my clothes at the Salvation Army. Their logic was it wasn't worth buying something brand new at full price since kids outgrow it in six months anyway. I get that. I agree with it. But the popular kids in my elementary school used my outdated style as fodder for picking on me. See, this was long before shopping at thrift stores became cool. It was back when second-hand meant you were tacky - or worse, poor.

The popular kids' parents bought them brand new outfits from Bradley's every year. They always looked great for school. The Amici twins wore matching outfits, except Nicole would wear a red or pink version while Lisa would wear the blue edition. Their hair, however, would always be done identically. Jennifer Sporello would dress in something complementary to the twins every day, as if their mothers went shopping together and then coordinated their outfits. It was so impressive! They were little style icons. Walking kids clothing commercials, while I was what-not-to-wear.

In second grade my mother bought me an adorable, brand new purple skirt from Osh Kosh B'gosh. It swirled out when I spun around and actu-

Down the Rabbit Hole

ally flattered my chubby figure. We got it on a rare trip to the outlet mall and I was so excited to wear it to school! I couldn't wait to show off my new item of clothing that had not been previously broken in by someone else my size.

I arrived at school feeling semi-confident. I was pretty sure my classmates were going to look twice at me today. Maybe even my crush, Anthony Rossi, would think I looked pretty. I'd had a crush on him since first grade, but he was going out with Nicole Amici, the most popular girl in our class. (Yes, they were going out. I don't know how it went down in your elementary school, but in mine we moved fast.)

Anyway, I arrived on the blacktop prepared to move up the social ladder. It was an overcast day, not unusual for Middletown, but the energy on the playground felt rougher somehow. As soon as I stepped onto school grounds I felt it. Like it was a full moon or something. The kids were more violent than usual. Rough housing instead of playing. Bullying instead of teasing. I hesitated. Then I stopped in my tracks. Should I ignore this ominous warning? I mean, it was just a feeling and I'd been taught to ignore those. I moved forward.

Down the Rabbit Hole

I arrived at the center of the blacktop. Kids swarmed around me like flies in a tornado. Then I felt it. A brief, cool draft as my skirt was lifted up from behind, exposing my underwear to all surrounding spectators.

"No!" I yelled as I spun around in time to see Kevin Wilson running away cackling. Directly behind me was a group of third and fourth graders standing in a huddle laughing. Humiliated, I smoothed my hands over the back of my skirt, assuring myself that it was covering my bum. But just as my hands relaxed another perpetrating bully repeated the crime.

"Stop it!" I yelled at DeShawn Washington, who ran from me laughing manically. The number of eggers-on had increased, as this had become a drive-by flashing game.

"Leave me alone!" I half-commanded, half-pleaded, my helplessness prompting fat tears to fall. This display of vulnerability only exacerbated the situation. A string of assailants followed, as if it had been choreographed by a nightmare. Another person ran past, flipping up my skirt, I spun towards him. Another person ran past, flipping up my skirt, I spun towards him. Another person ran past, flipping up my skirt, I spun towards him. The audience grew. The laughter amplified. My humiliation swelled. My hands were grasping my skirt hard, trying to keep it down, but that just made the bullies yank harder. They'd get it up, even if it

Down the Rabbit Hole

meant ripping it. After all, the approval of others is worth getting in trouble for. Things got blurry. Tears blurred my eyes. Insults and laughter blurred my ears. The feeling of being hated blurred my heart. My brain blurred it out in an attempt not to feel any of it.

I had come in to school minutes earlier hoping to be admired. Well, you make plans and God laughs. Here I was. In the center of a circle of my peers. The center of attention. I cried. Everyone laughed.

Finally the teachers emerged from their classrooms and blew their whistles.

"Break it up! Time to go inside!" Reluctantly the crowd did as instructed.

"She's wearing blue underwear," I heard a first grader gossip to another. It was the first clear sentence I'd heard since the roar of laughter and mocking had taken over. My heart skipped a beat. *Oh no! I'm wearing blue underwear?* I though, cursing myself.

"BLUE underwear!" another girl echoed, "haHA!" I walked alone toward my class.

Down the Rabbit Hole

"Did you see her underwear? It's BLUE!" I heard another girl exclaim to her friends, who exploded into laughter like a group of hyenas.

"Who wears BLUE underwear?!" a male voice chided, but I couldn't see who it was with my head so low. I tried to disappear.

"Hahaha!" Laughter attacked me from all directions.

I prayed for someone to comfort me. Anyone. A peer, a teacher. I needed to be allowed to cry. I wanted justice brought down upon everyone who'd participated. What had just happened to me wasn't right. It was very wrong. My young butt had been exposed to the whole school against my will. It was forceful and violent. I was powerless and helpless. I could not stop it and, as usual, no one who was in charge came to my aid. I was deep in a state of feeling sorry for myself. The mix of emotions was too powerful and overwhelming to feel all at once, so I just shut down.

Zombie-like I walked into my classroom. I heard snickering but was too zoned out to hear specific words. I took my seat and gradually began to emerge from my haze. The familiarity of my desk comforted me. School was about to begin and I could focus on that to distract me from obsessing about what had just happened. I reassured myself, or God assured me, that everything would be alright and I began to feel a little better.

Down the Rabbit Hole

This was the pattern of my abuse: being attacked from all angles, asking for help from responsible adults and not getting it, falling down the rabbit hole, then being reassured by God.

I looked up as Anthony Rossi walked into the room snickering to himself, "blue underwear." And again I sank. The boy who I'd wanted to notice me in a new, positive way was laughing at me.

When I got home from school I attempted to confide what had happened to my mother.

"That reminds me of a joke," she said. "A little girl goes to school in a short skirt that shows her underwear when she bends over. A boy walks up to her and says, *I bet you can't climb that really high tree over there!* She says, *I bet I can!* So she climbs it and when she gets back down he says, *Hey nice underwear!* When she gets home she tells her mom and her mom says, *Well that's what you get for wearing those short skirts!* So the next morning she goes to school in an even shorter skirt. The same guy comes over and says, *I bet you can't climb that really really high tree over there!* She says, *I bet I can!* So she climbs it and when she gets back down the boy has a stunned look on his face. She goes home and tells her mom, *I outsmarted him! Today I didn't wear any underwear!*"

Chapter 16 — Mom's Typical Overreaction

At seven years old and in the second grade, I was not on the bus route, so it was up to one of my hung-over parents to drive me to school every day. I cursed that fucking bus route. If I could've just taken the Goddamn bus I wouldn't even have to *see* my parents before school. They were, to put it mildly, um, not morning people. Unless you count two AM when they were royally fucked up. Then they were early morning people. But seven AM? Not so much. So every day that I made it to school began with two angry, impatient adults yelling at me. As if school were an extracurricular activity and they were doing me a favor. Although, I did love the mandatory excuse to get out of my house. But anyway.

On this particular morning my dad was on the road with a show, so it was just us three girls in the small house on Bixby street. My mother awoke unhappy. She was so groggy that I worried it might end up being yet another day I didn't make it to school. Funny how, on those days, she'd tell them *I* was sick, when it was clearly *her* that needed medical attention. But today she dragged her sorry ass out of bed and schlepped to the car. Barely able to see, she resentfully began the half mile drive to Farm Hill Elementary School, with me unbelted in the back seat.

Down the Rabbit Hole

"Get out and get me a newspaper," she commanded, suddenly swerving over to the side of the road. She tossed a quarter at me and I jumped out of the car to obey. I knew she was in a huge hurry to get back to bed and anything that postponed her nap by even a second would set her off. I ran across the street and threw the twenty-five cent piece in the slot of the newspaper box. I then noticed that the box was empty… just a split second too late. There were no more Middletown Presses left. I started to quiver with anxiety. My eyes darted to a nearby house. *Maybe I can ask the people in there for a quarter and sneak back before mom notices. Hell, maybe I can ask them to adopt me and escape this hell permanently.* Anything would be better than returning to my mother sans quarter or newspaper.

I cautiously began my walk back across the street, looking carefully both ways for oncoming traffic. *Maybe I'll get hit by a car and my mother will feel bad and forget about the quarter,* I thought optimistically. *We'll hafta go to the hospital, she'll realize how lucky she is that I'm still alive, she'll vow to be a better mother and we'll all live happily ever after!* But unfortunately the street was clear.

"There were no more papers," I singsonged, as if to say, *Oh well.*

"Give me my quarter back," she demanded. Fuck.

Down the Rabbit Hole

"I, uh, I don't have it."

She looked over her shoulder, demanding an explanation with her death stare.

"I had already put in the slot before I noticed it was empty." I said apologetically.

"You WHAT!?!" she exploded.

That was it. Her excuse to take her anger out on me was now fully set in motion, and entirely justifiable to her alcoholic brain. She turned and began to wallop me repeatedly, craning herself to reach me in the back seat. I covered my face and began to cry.

"You stupid idiot! You Goddamned stupid stupid child!" she kept repeating, one word per whack. She was especially strong this morning.

"I'm sorry! I'm sorry!" I repeated sincerely. And I was. I felt stupid and ashamed. But somewhere, deep down, I knew this was an overreaction. It was, after all, a quarter we were talking about. Any adult could've accidentally inserted the coin before noticing the bin was empty. It was an honest, inconsequential, meaningless mistake. But Denise did not see it that way. And she was the adult here. Technically, anyway.

When her arm got tired she shifted her anger to the gas pedal. Peeling out of her makeshift spot, she sped down the residential street. I was thrown back by the force and tried to grab onto anything to keep from falling sideways. I steadied myself and scooted nearer to the door so I would be a little further out of her reach if she chose to turn around and hit me again. We sharply peeled left, blowing through a stop sign as if we were in a video game. My head hit the window and I grasped at the seat to balance.

Up ahead I saw another stop sign with three kids about to walk their bikes across the street. I wished she would've hit them. Then she would've gone to jail and everyone would know what a monster she was. I'd be put in a foster home and everything would finally be ok. But she did not hit them. She sped up to the stop sign, then slammed on the brakes. The same move she scolded my father for every time he came to a stop. I decided not to mention that. The kids looked scared.

"Come on! MOVE!" she yelled at them.

Down the Rabbit Hole

They looked unsure of what to do. Should they trust this crazy woman not to hit them if they crossed the street? I crouched down so they could not identify me, but peeked to see if I knew them. Thankfully I did not. At least there was that.

"GO! GO!" she continued to scream. "I'll run 'em all over then turn on the wipers to clean their splattered blood off the windshield!" she threatened. "I don't care!" The three kids cautiously, slowly crossed the street, looking quizzically at this maniac screaming from her car. *Hurry up!* I cursed them silently. *Why are you moving so slow!? Don't you realize that the slower you move, the more I pay for it later!?* I hated kids who didn't know how to quickly obey my parents. They made it so much worse for me.

We rounded the corner to my school and I knew, for the next few hours, I was safe. I jumped out of the car. Wiping my tears and straightening my clothes, I put on my 'everything's ok' face and walked inside. I heard my mother's tires squeal as she peeled away. Although my fellow classmates and teachers took notice of this noisy departure, I did not look back. I pretended not to know the car that was leaving its mark in burnt rubber.

Down the Rabbit Hole

Chapter 17 — Breakfast Coke

For the first five years of my sister's life I was her mother. I got her up in the morning. I dressed her and got her breakfast. I brushed her teeth and her hair. And I made sure she stayed very quiet, so as not to wake my parents.

One morning when I was eight and my sister three, I hurried through this AM routine, then scurried back to my room to hide. You see, I was afraid my parents would wake up and emerge from their room to see the cocaine they'd left on the kitchen table the night before.

They were usually good about keeping their hard drugs hidden. I knew what they were doing behind their bedroom door, though I'd never seen their stash. I'd watch them from my bed as they'd go into their room twice or three times a night. They'd open their top drawer, hide behind the slightly ajar door, scrape a razor across a mirror, then inhale quickly and deeply. I'd looked in that drawer during the day, but all I found was paraphernalia: a wooden keepsake box, a mirror, a razor and straw clipping. The drugs themselves they must've either hidden elsewhere or finished each night.

Down the Rabbit Hole

But this night they must've forgotten to clean up their evidence. Because there it sat in plain view of my sister as she ate her cereal. A pink make-up mirror with two lines of white powder, a snippet of a straw and a razor blade sat in the center of the kitchen table. I thought about moving it to the counter so my sister didn't have to stare at it, but I didn't dare touch it. Instead I went back to my room and hid, pretending I hadn't seen anything. I didn't want my parents to find both my sister and I sitting staring at their wrongdoings. So I just laid in my bed and waited, terrified. I was sure I was going to get yelled at.

"Did you see that?" she'd scream before striking me across the face. "Did you touch it? Don't you dare tell anybody or I'll kill you!"

I lay envisioning the terrible abuse that I was about to endure. And I felt for my poor sister, who sat a few feet away crunching her cocoa pebbles while staring at this poison. I was sure she also knew what it was, and I was sure she was being traumatized by being in its toxic presence. But I was frozen in fear. I didn't know what else to do.

A few moments later my mother came out of her room. My heart began to race. She burped loudly and shuffled to the kitchen. Then she spotted the drugs she'd mistakenly left behind the night before.

Down the Rabbit Hole

"Oh my God!" she screamed and burst into tears. "Eddie!" she cried, and my father appeared. I listened as my mother cried and hugged my sister. "I'm so sorry!" she wailed. My father remained silent, picked up the evidence, and put it away in their top drawer. My mother, holding my sister, stumbled into my room and hugged me. "I'm so sorry! I'm so sorry you had to see that!" she cried, tears streaming down her face. This was not the reaction I had been expecting at all! She felt bad?

"It's ok," I repeated, for that's all I knew how to say. It's ok, it's ok, it's ok. Whatever trauma you've inflicted upon me, it's ok. I'll be ok. Don't feel bad. Everything is ok.

My mother put my sister down and went into her room with my father. She closed the door. We remained silent, unsure of what to do next. I heard them talking, but could not make out what they were saying. I imagined they were *again* talking about how they had to change their lives. How *this* was their wake up call and they could not continue to subject their children to this life of trauma anymore. I fantasized that they made a solid promise to become better parents from *that* moment forward. To give up the drugs and drinking and make their children their number one priority. I hoped. I wished. I prayed.

Down the Rabbit Hole

A few moments passed before they emerged from their room once again. I had not moved from the bottom bunk, but now Sibby laid with me. We cuddled together, feeling alone. They approached and crouched down.

"Hi Punkie," my father said in his phony voice. This was the voice he used when he knew he'd done something wrong, but did not know how to apologize for it. Higher pitched, feminine, soft, delicate. He stroked my hair. "I'm so sorry you had to see that."

"It's ok," I repeated.

"I love you, baby." He kissed my head. "I love you both very much." He wrapped his arms around us. "Do you wanna go to Gumma and Da's?"

"Yes," I answered. They couldn't face us. The shame was too much to handle. But I fantasized that they wanted to check into rehab. I hoped that they were going to follow through on my previous fantasy that *this* was the impetus they needed to change.

The four of us drove to Gumma and Da's silently, except for the sound of Rush Limbaugh's brainwashing. I remained helpless, alone, and sad up in my head until I felt the safety of my grandparents' presence.

Down the Rabbit Hole

I did not tell my grandparents what had happened that morning. The event gradually decreased in importance as I played on my bike with my friends who lived across the street. It travelled to the very back of my mind as we ate McDonald's in the corner booth for dinner. I forgot it entirely as Gumma sang "Chattanooga Choo Choo" while pulling me by the leg as we crawled up the stairs to bed. The traumatizing morning was erased by night, as my grandparents made everything better. Everything really was going to be ok.

The following year the first national tour of *Les Miserables* took us to Philadelphia. We lived in a ghetto apartment in Bensalem, a cheap suburb, where our neighbors became my parents' drug buddies. Even at nine years old I knew this young couple were drug addicts just by looking at them. They were unnaturally happy. They smiled a lot, because they were looking forward to the high that was coming. They wore old, worn clothing. Their hair and teeth needed attention. They didn't seem to ever leave their apartment. These became my parents lower companions.

They never hung out with my parents during the day. In fact I don't ever remember them coming over socially. But when we'd run into them in the hallway I could tell they spent a lot of time with my parents after we kids went to bed. They were clearly using buddies. Perhaps dealers.

Down the Rabbit Hole

One night my mother was annihilated, as usual. My father was not home from work yet. My sister and I were asleep in our room. The neighbors must've been passed out next door because my mother was alone. Just her, her drinks and her drugs. Since she did her best thinking at this time, she called me out of my slumber to soberly witness her drunken genius. I was afraid, of course, because her calling me out into the living room was her calling me to the head of the line of fire. It was never going to go well. I rounded the corner into the living room/dining room area and found my mother, feeling bold and brave, sitting at the kitchen table behind a mirror of cocaine. My mind flashed back to the breakfast table only a short year before. How sorry she'd been for me having seen this, yet here she was now calling me in to have a chat over it. Well, perhaps she felt like having a mother/daughter bonding moment. This was surely something we could laugh about now. "Haha! Remember that time Sibby ate breakfast with this stuff?! Classic!" But no such luck.

"Sit," she instructed. I cautiously obeyed, taking the seat opposite her at the dining room table. Her eyes were bloodshot, her nose beet red. I'd seen my mother drunk before, many times, but this night she was clearly deep in a blackout. "You're worthless," she spat. "You're fat and ugly. You'll never amount to anything."

Down the Rabbit Hole

I started to cry silently, for I was in a hopeless situation. She was so drunk she didn't know what she was saying, and she wouldn't cop to remembering any of this in the morning.

What had I done to deserve this, I wondered? I'd been a good daughter, a good sister, a good person. Why did God find it necessary to keep punishing me? Why, of all people, did I deserve this abuse? I wished my father would come home. He'd be sober, so he'd save me.

I sat in silence as Denise picked up the small piece of straw on the mirror. She put one finger on her nostril, the straw up her other nostril, then sniffed in a full, thick line of cocaine. I was amazed she could coordinate this endeavor, seeing as how drunk she was. Her eyes and mouth turned condescending.

"You'll never be an actress. Look at how fat you are!" Of course any dreams I had expressed out loud would eventually be used against me. I felt myself detaching, going elsewhere. Someplace safe inside my own head. I began to talk to myself in my head. *Like she's some big prize. Look at her! Jesus Christ! Somebody beat her with the drunk and ugly stick! How could she possibly be insulting me!?* My thoughts made me smile internally and I felt a little better. Like everything would be ok if I could keep a sense of humor going. My mother continued for a little bit, repeating herself and feeling superior. And I continued to reply internally and feel better than her. Eventually she dismissed me with her catch-phrase.

"Get out of my sight."

I laid in my bed, unable to sleep. I was triggered, but trying to console myself with humorous thoughts. I heard my father come home and she started right in with him. The cocaine had given her fuel and she was ready for a fight. I heard her lunge at him and he caught her and threw her to the ground. *Yeah!* I thought, *Get her!*

"Are you out of your fucking mind!?" He whisper-yelled, so as not to wake us. She must've lost her enthusiasm for the fight then, because I couldn't hear anything else in detail. Eventually the lights went out in the other room and they went to bed, together. How my dad could get into bed with a woman who'd just tried to attack him is beyond me, but he did.

The next morning I awoke before anyone. The cocaine was still on the table, as if my parents thought, "fuck it." I sat on the couch and turned the TV on low. After an hour or so my parents emerged from their room. My mother saw the cocaine and beckoned my father. He picked it up and

Down the Rabbit Hole

took it into their room. No one said anything. There were no apologies. Just an elephant in the room for us to ignore.

Chapter 18 — *Les Miserables*

My father worked automation on the first national tour of *Les Miserables* from its inception in 1987 to its close in 1991. I was eight years old when we began touring and it was my dream to play little Cosette. The logo on the *Les Miz* attire was little Cosette's face and I'd get asked constantly if I was the little girl on my jacket, t-shirt, sweatshirt. Sadly, I'd answer no. But I wanted to be.

"You're too fat. Cosette is supposed to be starving," my mother would reason.

One night, while on a six month stop in Virginia, my parents asked me to sing "Castle on a Cloud" to them. My mother had brought up the idea to my father that perhaps they *should* allow me to audition. This was to be be my audition to audition.

I entered the living room in character, took my seated position on the floor, legs to my side, leaning on my arms, and began to sing. I was nervous, for this would be my most critical audience ever, but I didn't let it show. I sang with heartfelt emotion. I knew what it was like to be a little girl trapped in a home where no one wanted her. Used for her cleaning skills and as a babysitter to her sibling. I could go there easily. I sang without accompaniment and when I was done I felt good about what I had done.

"You can't really hit the low notes," my mother said.

"I know, but that doesn't happen when I'm singing to the tapes. I think maybe I just went too low because I'm singing without music."

"Yeah," she agreed. She nodded a few times, then turned to my father. "I think we should let her audition," she said. My heart soared. I got so excited I thought I might cry.

"Yeah..." he answered skeptically. "But I don't want you to be upset if you don't get it." Reality smacked me back down.

"I won't be," I promised.

"If you really wanna be an actress you're gonna have to get used to hearing no a lot," he continued, as if he knew firsthand what he was talking about.

"I know," I said obediently, as if I did too.

Down the Rabbit Hole

I went to bed skeptical. Too wise-to-their-tricks to allow myself to get excited. My mother loved pulling the rug out from under me. I wouldn't be surprised, or allow her to see I was affected, if she did it again.

Still... what if they actually *did* allow me to audition? And what if I got the part! I fantasized, against my better judgement, that I became the touring Little Cosette. That directors and actors and audiences and critics praised me so much that my parents had no choice but to confirm my talents. I'd be swept up by the biggest agents and begged to play the child with the emotional arc in every production. Too busy for my parents to handle, but too famous for them to take me out of it, I'd use my own money to support myself, leave my abusive home, and go on to live out my Katrina and Katerina fantasy. It could happen... It really could...

The following morning I feared leaving my room. I'd let myself dream big, so I had a long fall if my fears were confirmed. As long as I didn't see my parents I could still believe that my dream of auditioning for Little Cosette could come true. If I didn't give them the opportunity, they couldn't take it away from me. Perhaps I could stay in my room all day long. Maybe my dad would leave for work, my mother would get on with her chores, and by the time tomorrow comes around their plans to renege on me would turn to indifference. They'd say, "oh, whatever. Audition if you want, we don't care," and I could go on to get the part.

"KATE!" My mother's annoyed voice bellowed from the living room. *Whelp. There goes that idea*, I thought, crestfallen. "It's 1 o'clock in the afternoon! What the hell were you doing in there?" Denise accused.

"Nothing," I replied automatically.

"Get your sister dressed. We've got errands to run," she commanded.

My heart resumed its normal pace as I went about the mundane activities of a mother, realizing that my own had forgotten about the previous night's audition. *Maybe she's forgotten all about it, and I can gently remind her the night before the auditions. I'll be sure to catch her at a good time, so she won't say no. This could still work…*

Two days went by. My hopes rose to the top. On the third night my mother, wasted out of her mind, called me out to the living room where she sat with my equally-as-intoxicated father.

"We're not gonna let you audition," she slurred. My foggy eyed father let a wry smile creep across his face, as if he took pleasure in watching me accept this painful news. "You're not gonna get it, so what's the point?" She explained.

I turned and left the room. Unwilling to let them see that my feelings were hurt, that I felt my dreams were being crushed, that they had won. I put on my strong face and went to bed.

It's OK, I told myself, or God assured me, over and over again. *It's fine. As soon as you're able to drive you're gonna audition and get huge parts! They can't take your dreams away from you. They can only delay them a little. You are going to become stronger as a result of this.* My inner God voice comforted me until I fell asleep.

Chapter 19 — Plaster Victim

My father is a rageaholic. Take his mode of summoning me, for example. He'd start soft.

"Ka-ate..." Too soft to hear unless I was listening for it.

Then he'd increase to normal call volume, "Ka-ate!"

Then, if I didn't reply instantly, he'd escalate to one hundred: "KATE!!!"

I should always be on edge, see. I should always be prepared to come running. Even if it is just to the dinner table.

Like a drill sergeant, he thinks fear is the best teacher. Maybe that's why I'm so smart. I was always afraid of him.

When my sister and I shared a room in our small house on Bixby street we often bickered. But we learned quickly to put our differences aside if my father was home, because if he heard us fighting he'd storm in and scare the fight out of both of us. He saw our disagreements as an opportunity to outlet his own anger. He could scream and hit us, thus relieving

Down the Rabbit Hole

some of his pent-up rage, meanwhile disguising his outburst as a lesson teaching us to "get along." And it worked. By the end of my father's thirty second visits to our room, my sister and I were inevitably holding and soothing each other.

One day when I was around eight and my sister around three we were playing in our room. Although my sister was too young to really get mad at, we began to fight over something. A crayon? A doll? Who knows. But I got frustrated.

"Sibby!" I whined. "Give me that! It's mine!"

My mischievous sister fought back. "No!" she whined, pulling back.

Out of nowhere, our door swung open and the doorknob went through our wall. My father, enraged, eyes like bloodshot saucers, bellowed, "SHUT THE FUCK UP!" then slammed the door shut, pulling shards of plaster along with it and exposing a new doorknob-shaped hole in the wall.

My sister and I grabbed each other in a tearful hug and shushed each other's sobs. Whatever anger we had had at each other evaporated and was quickly replaced by fear of our enraged father.

Down the Rabbit Hole

We whispered to each other, "I'm sorry, Sibby."

"I'm sorry Punkie."

"I love you."

We shook in fear. Would he come back? Were we being quiet enough now?

My mother entered a few minutes later.

"What the fuck?" she exclaimed, examining the hole in the wall that she'd clearly been informed of. "Look what you made your father do!" She scolded us with a tone that warned that we were now in trouble for his accidental property damage. "Oh, you're gonna get it!" She threatened, supporting my father's anger.

As I often did when I felt sad and alone, I climbed into my bed. It was mid-afternoon, but I lay in my top bunk and pulled down the shade. I didn't know what else to do. I was too afraid to leave my room. So I just tried to escape into my dreams.

Down the Rabbit Hole

The next day my father came into our room with a bucket of spackle and a putty knife. As I lay in my bed he proceeded to fix his physical mistake. Neither one of us said a thing. It was a long, awkward silence. I felt full of fear. What was he thinking? What was to come? His silence was deafening. Not knowing what he was thinking and feeling made me feel isolated. I tried to read his mind. Out of the corner of my eye I watched him. His Mona Lisa face told me he felt nothing. No remorse, guilt, or shame. When he was done he left and shut the door. I closed my eyes and tried to sleep my nightmarish life away.

Down the Rabbit Hole

Chapter 20 — *Mommy Dearest*

For some reason *Mommy Dearest* was always playing on our TV. Seriously. That shit was on all the time. It was the movie of the week for years, it seemed, so it was constantly inappropriately interrupted by commercials. Who's in charge of where to insert commercials when they play movies on TV? I think that person must get such a kick out of putting a douche commercial right after Faye Dunaway beats the hell out of her daughter. *Tension breaker! The audience could use a laugh right about now.*

Anyway, I liked that movie. It was familiar, except for all the richness and the big mansion and the crazy doll collection and stuff. Other than that, there was a lot I could relate to. Bat shit crazy mom beating her daughter with wire hangers; drunken, compulsive three AM gardening. You know, the yoush. But I envied the daughter in that movie because, although she was abused, she had a really nice room. I wanted that canopy bed! And all that space! And a nanny! At least she had a nanny to mother her. And then she got to go off to college and have sex in a horse stall! Lucky bitch. THEN she got to exploit her trauma through spoken word. Ideal! That's the kind of alcoholic upbringing I wanted. If I couldn't have a fairy tale life, let's at least modify the one I have to make it a little less pathet-

Down the Rabbit Hole

ic. I mean Jesus Christ, what a white trash, train wreck main character my mother was! Why couldn't she at least get up hungover at the ass crack of dawn and run five miles to keep it tight for the cameras!? My mother rolled out of bed at noon for a quick cigarette and a faded, plastic McDonalds cup of ice water before passing out again, until it was time to drink. My house was the opposite of glamorous. It was an embarrassment.

I ended up watching part of *Mommy Dearest* with my mother one day and she said the funniest thing. She said, "you're lucky I don't make you call me that." It was funny because I had been sitting there, on the couch next to my mother, thinking *well, this could be good that we're watching this together. Maybe she'll see the similarities between her own behavior and Joan Crawford's. Maybe it'll be some kind of wake up call for her. Maybe she'll feel a little guilty because she recognizes this crazy alcoholic behavior in herself. Maybe she'll feel a little bad and put her arm around me and tell me she loves me. That'd be enough right now. Baby steps. Just a little self-realization. Enough to make today a good day. Enough to temper her temper just for today.* But she had not been thinking along those lines at all. She had been on her own sick path in her own sick head thinking of how she wasn't that bad in comparison. Funny how you can be sitting right next to someone, thinking you're sharing an energy, a moment, a thought, and turns out all along you were alone in that feeling. They weren't feeling that way at all.

I felt a responsibility to laugh off comments such as those, so I snarfed and brushed it off. Kind of like, "Ha! Yeah... I AM lucky you don't make me call you mommy dearest. THAT would be child abuse!"

Down the Rabbit Hole

Chapter 21 — Similarities

Nicole and Lisa Amici, the twins in my grade, bullied me one day, then friended me the next. Desperate for acceptance, I abided this crazy behavior and looked forward to the days when they decided I was cool. I was lonely and they were popular. Christ, if *anyone* was nice to me I'd've forgiven them their trespassing no matter how demoralizing and played along like nothing had ever happened.

One hot afternoon I was invited to the twins' house after school to play. I was so excited to be invited by myself! Not a birthday party or a group of friends, but just the three of us. Maybe they were beginning to see me as an equal. At the very least they were treating me as one temporarily. We spent the better part of the afternoon playing hide and seek and tag. When we got tired we decided it was time for a snack. Nicole got a brand new bag of Oreos out of her cupboard and Lisa poured us each a cup of milk. Nicole drank half of hers immediately, then poured the remainder down the drain. *What a waste!* I thought, hearing my father's voice bellowing in my brain. *I'd get reamed if I threw away half a glass of milk! We hadn't even eaten a single cookie yet. Hasn't she thought of that? She'll be wishing she had that milk in a few minutes when her mouth is dry from cookie dust.*

Down the Rabbit Hole

We took our snacks out onto the deck. Lisa pulled the sliding glass door shut behind us. The bright sun hit it in such a way that the inside disappeared and we could see our reflections in the glass.

"Hey," Nicky said, "dare me to throw a cookie at the patio door?" I loved dares when I didn't have to do them.

"Yes!" I squealed. Lisa remained silent. Without hesitation Nicky turned and pitched an Oreo at the glass. She threw with medium strength as if she was trying to impress me by being daring, but still trying to appear innocent should she get caught. "It slipped out of my hand," I could imagine her saying to her mother, who'd come out to investigate the noise.

The cookie broke and fell to the wooden floor. Nicky began to walk towards it to pick up the evidence when, without missing a beat, Mrs. Amici pulled open the patio door, grabbed Nicky by the wrist and began hitting her. *What!?* I thought. *Mrs. Amici hits the twins?* Usually tough Nicky covered her head and started to cry like a baby.

"I'm sorry! I'm sorry!" she whined, reminding me of myself, helplessly begging her mother to stop hitting her.

Down the Rabbit Hole

Mrs. Amici pulled Nicky inside and slammed the sliding glass door shut to continue the beating in private. I turned to look at Lisa, who was upset, but not surprised. Her look told me that this was not the first time Nicky had been hit, and her body language suggested that she too had been the victim of some physical discipline as well. She sat on the edge of the picnic table, almost as if she were preparing to take off in a sprint. She looked small, younger than she was. She was down the rabbit hole. I knew that place well. *Maybe we're not so different after all,* I thought. I was comforted by this newfound knowledge. It blew my mind to learn that even the most popular kids in school were made to feel powerless by their older, stronger relatives. I suddenly felt equal to the twins instead of inferior, as I'd always felt before.

A few moments later Mrs. Amici came back out to the patio.

"Kate, call your mother to come pick you up," she said.

I obeyed. I walked inside and picked up the phone in the kitchen. Nicole was nowhere in sight. I listened for her cries, but heard nothing. Lisa began up the stairs.

Down the Rabbit Hole

"Lisa, leave Nicole alone!" Mrs. Amici ordered. Lisa turned and descended the stairs again, a crestfallen look on her face. *She's even denying Nicky the comfort of another human being,* I thought. *She's really mad.*

As I sat in the kitchen waiting for Denise to arrive, I took note of Mrs. Amici's behavior. She was seething, but trying to maintain some of her cool. She huffed around the living room and kitchen slamming things down, up in her angry head thinking about how she'd unload onto Mr. Amici when he got home. He could take it from here. She'd had enough. I followed her thoughts. What would Mr. Amici do to Nicky? I was sure she'd get a good beating, now that I knew the Amicis were into that sort of thing. She'd probably also get grounded, or some other typical type of punishment. But would her dad get drunk and tell her she drove him to it? Would Mrs. Amici come upstairs in the middle of the night to finish beating Nicky while in the midst of a drug-fueled blackout? The possibilities were endless to me now that I'd seen how this family behaves in their own home. They could be exactly like Ed and Denise, only better dressed.

I suddenly felt taller. More confident. I was equal to the popular girls in a way that mattered more to me than outward appearances. Their insides were damaged too. They knew that triggered place, that I so often went to alone. The rabbit hole I thought only unpopular kids fell down. A helpless, powerless, lonely place inside our heads. We shared that lonely space, so I was no longer alone.

Down the Rabbit Hole

Chapter 22 — MY Father Knows Best

The cast and crew of *Les Miz* went to a baseball game together one Monday on their collective day off. Because my parents leapt at any opportunity to ditch us, they left me at home to babysit Sibby while they went to the park together.

Stellan, one of the actors, had a son named Liam. He was a few years younger than me at the time, so I'm guessing he was around seven. When they entered the ball park, Stellan bought Liam an inflatable baseball bat as a souvenir. They found their seats in the stadium and my father wound up sitting next to Liam. As kids do, Liam played with his toy, waving it around in the air, while his father, who sat on the other side of him, ignored his play and partook in conversation with a co-worker. Well, my father was all business. He was there to watch the game, God damnit.

"Stop waving that thing in my face," my father claims he fairly warned Liam, twice. But apparently the child did not obey, and Stellan remained oblivious to the distraction. So, in typical Edward Russell fashion, upon the third incident of the neon balloon slightly obstructing his view, my "fair" father exploded in anger and tore the toy from the boy's hands.

Down the Rabbit Hole

"YOU LITTLE SHIT! IF YOU DON'T STOP WAVING THIS FUCKING THING IN MY FACE I'M GONNA SHOVE IT STRAIGHT UP YOUR ASS!" That got his father's attention. Liam exploded in tears.

"Oh honey, he didn't mean it!" My father claims Stellan coddled his son, lifting him up and hugging away the fear.

"My ass, I didn't mean it!" Ed stubbornly defended. Liam continued to cry, overdramatizing the moment and begging for more babying from his weak father.

"I warned him to stop waving that thing in my face," my father would reiterate the many times he retold this story, as if that were sufficient justification for his outburst. He remained convinced that he was right. Exploding on a seven year old was *unquestionably* the right way to act in that situation and he sure as hell didn't owe anyone an apology. Not Stellan, who never spoke to him again. Not my mother, who silently sat next to him, ashamed, but afraid to say anything. Certainly not that spoiled little shit who dared wave a harmless toy in my father's line of vision. No. Edward Russell, as usual, was right. If only everyone would behave the way he thought they should. Then he wouldn't be forced to burst out in fits of rage in public. Didn't people see that? If they weren't so stupid they

Down the Rabbit Hole

would see that he was right one hundred percent of the time and get in line! Don't they know who he thinks he is! It's ALL about him, people. He is the center of the universe and if you get in his way it's your ass, and you should know better.

Lest anyone think he was the least bit sorry for his actions, my father would tell and re-tell this story with pride to reinforce that his short-tempered parenting style was, not only justified, but correct.

Yeah... I'm really glad I missed that outing.

Down the Rabbit Hole

Chapter 23 — A Peek Inside The Chaos

As unwilling as my Gumma might've been to outwardly admit that her son might have a drinking problem, deep down both she and my Da knew it was true. One day when I was nine years old, my Da came to pick us up from our little house on Bixby street. For whatever unacceptable reason my parents were not home and my sister and I were left alone. It was rare for Gumma or Da to enter the house on Bixby street. I think they knew that if they saw the chaos, the filth, the obvious signs of dysfunction, they'd be forced to recognize that the son they'd tried so hard to raise to be a moral man had fallen short. But on this day, Da came to the door to retrieve us. I let him inside while I gathered my sister and her diaper bag from our room. When I returned to the kitchen with everything in tow I caught Da looking in my parents' liquor cabinet. He didn't hear me approach so for about twenty seconds I got to see his genuine concern as he took out the jugs, one by one, to examine the remaining liquid inside. Though his back was to me, I could tell by his body language that he was concerned. He moved bottles aside to peer into the deep cabinet, full of back up bottles. He took note of the many liters of tonic and seltzer water that aligned the left hand side of the wooden cabinet. He sighed, then caught me staring out of the corner of his eye. Quickly he put down the almost empty gallon jug of vodka he'd been holding and shut the cabinet door.

"Ready to go?" he asked me hopefully. I felt sad. I didn't want him to ignore his discovery. I wanted him to ask me about my parents' drinking. I wanted that can of worms opened. But I took his cue and simply replied, "yes."

Once in the car, however, Da became unable to hold his tongue.

"Do your parents drink every night?" he asked me, his far off gaze suggested that he was deep in thought, not quite aware that he was prompting a child for inside information.

"Yes," I blurted out, so relieved to reveal this painful secret. "They both drink every night. They get so drunk and they fight. They hit me and each other."

I began sobbing and Da began to withdraw. He was absolutely not prepared for this barrage of upsetting information.

"It's awful," I continued. "I wish I could just live with you and Gumma forever!"

Down the Rabbit Hole

I wiped the tears from my face and waited for Da to tell me everything was going to be all right. That I could stay with him and Gumma until my parents cleaned up their act. That he and Gumma would save me from the hell I was trapped in. But he remained silent. Long gone into his own thoughts. Preoccupied with whatever his head was telling him. Seemingly oblivious to my pain. I stopped crying and joined his silence, venturing into my own thoughts. *I've said too much,* I regretted. *He doesn't want to hear all this bad stuff about his son. I should've just left it at yes and let him ask more questions if he wanted to know more.* We traveled the rest of the way in silence.

Down the Rabbit Hole

Chapter 24 — Walking Pneumonia

My parents smoked cigarettes like it was their job. Two packs a day each of Barclay box and Marlboro Mediums, our house was one big ashtray. My sister and I breathed second hand smoke all day every day. My mother wore the stale odor of cigarettes like a perfume. My father's breath was tobacco-scented. Their teeth were yellow and they coughed every few seconds. My father began most sentences with, "aah-HA," loud and startling. My mother cleared her phlegmy throat, which turned into a cough, "aah-ehh-eh-eh-eh-eh... cough, cough." It was their theme song. They smoked in bed, waking up in the middle of the night for a cigarette, while the other slept soundly through the wafting toxic fumes. They smoked in the car, window cracked just enough to flick ash out of it. My father even smoked while playing baseball on his stagehand's league. Both hands on the bat, cig dangling from his lips. Smoking accompanied everything they did. I equated second-hand smoke with discomfort. It was a familiar smell, in a bad way.

One day while living in the ghetto that is Bensalem, Pennsylvania I got sick. Flu-like symptoms: throwing up, fever, chills, coughing. My unsympathetic mother dismissed my sickness, and continued to drink and snort coke in the living room with her music on full blast as I lay on the bathroom floor next to the toilet.

On the third day of my worsening illness my mother finally took me to the ER. What started out as a chest cold had turned into walking pneumonia. My lungs were filled with fluid and had to be "tapped." I was admitted to the hospital and hooked up to an IV. Because I was too weak to operate on, I had to stay in the hospital for nine days until I regained some strength.

I woke up on the second day surrounded by lobby shop gifts: a Radar, Big Bird's teddy bear from *Sesame Street;* a basket of flowers and a mylar balloon that read "get well soon." On one hand, I felt sad that my parents hadn't woken me up to say hello. On the other, I was glad to have missed them.

Two days later I switched on the wall-mounted TV. Thirteen channels of nothing. One channel was just a surveillance camera of the hospital church. Sadly, that was the most interesting channel. I kept it on so I could watch people scarcely come in and kneel at the alter to pray. There was no sound, but I imagined they prayed for their sick loved ones who were upstairs. Everyone crossed themselves, keeping their heads bowed humbly. I wished my parents had a faith. Their lack of humility was staggering. If only they weren't so narcissistic, maybe they could believe there was something bigger than themselves out there.

I fell back asleep and woke up as the sun was setting and my mom, dad and sister were coming in.

"Hi Punkie," they cooed, hugging me gently and kissing me on the head.

"You got your teddy bear?" my mother nudged, seeking a thank you.

"Yes, thank you," I obeyed. "Why didn't you wake me?" I asked.

"The nurse told us not to," my father lied. "What are you watching?" he asked judgmentally, changing the subject. The TV was still on the Chapel channel.

"Nothing," I said, embarrassed. He clicked it off.

"How are you feeling?" my father asked.

"A little better, but still really weak."

"Are you able to eat anything?"

Down the Rabbit Hole

"No. I threw up water earlier."

"You gotta get better, Punkie," my father urged, as if it were my choice.

"I'm trying," I said. After a few minutes, my mother was getting restless.

"Where do you want to eat?" she asked my father under her breath, so I wouldn't hear them making plans without me. It must be Monday, I reasoned. My father would take us out to dinner on Monday nights.

"Wanna do Bennigans?" he answered. With their itinerary set, they excused themselves, gathered their things and left me alone in my hospital bed.

The next day my Da hurried into my room. Having heard about me being in the hospital, he had dropped everything and driven to Bensalem from Connecticut.

"Da!" I exclaimed. He hugged and kissed me with the empathy and love that unfortunately had not been passed down to my father.

"I'm so glad to see you," he said with relief.

Down the Rabbit Hole

My parents walked in behind him, their faces smug as if they had brought me this present. Turned out, when my father finally got around to telling his father that I was in the hospital Da *bought* a new car from the local Chevrolet dealer and drove to Pennsylvania. So hurriedly, in fact, that he left my grandmother behind, as she had been at work when he received the news. Promising to go back and get her, he just had to see me without any further delay. He stayed with me the rest of the day. Sitting in a chair next to my bed, he held my hand and petted my hair until I fell asleep. That night he left to drive back to Connecticut to get Gumma. The next afternoon they walked in together. I've never felt more loved.

Gumma and Da got a hotel room close to the hospital. I didn't have the kind of family that would automatically stay together during visits. I had the kind of family with lots to hide from each other. I'm sure my mother didn't offer to let her in-laws stay with them. There was no fucking way she was gonna modify her nightly routine. Then again, it wouldn't have mattered anyway. Gumma and Da would never have taken her up on the offer.

Gumma had never approved of my mother. She was white trash and not nearly good enough for my father. She couldn't keep house and never ironed our clothes. She left the house looking like a ragamuffin in her uniform of jeans, a tee shirt and sneakers.

Gumma rarely came inside the house on Bixby street, but I'm sure she'd painted a picture of it in her mind which greatly trumped the reality. However, since she and Da were here now, they were forced to visit our crack den apartment in Bensalem out of geographic obligation.

Visiting the apartment we were temporarily living in, Gumma saw things as they actually were. A shithole basement apartment completely undecorated and purposefully kept dark. The dusty aroma of ashtrays and alcohol everywhere, no effort to make it inviting. They feigned smiles and looked for something nice to say, then excused themselves as quickly as possible to escape the pigsty.

When they arrived back at the hospital after their forced visit I could tell by Gumma and Da's body language that they were disturbed. See, my mother didn't see a problem with the way she lived. She tried to play good daughter-in-law and invite her in-laws into her crack den with a phony smile and open veiny arms. But I could see through the thick fog of drugs to what my proper grandparents saw and I agreed, it was a train wreck. They walked into my hospital room ahead of my mother and Sib-

Down the Rabbit Hole

by. Their bodies and lips were stiff. They were not smiling. I could tell by their walk exactly what they'd just seen and what they were now thinking.

Take me home with you, I willed. *You're right, it's no place for a child to live. It's not safe and it is the reason I'm in here.*

Gumma and Da took their seats, one on each side of me, and remained tight lipped until my mother excused herself and my sister with some bullshit excuse about how she wanted to give Gumma and Da time to visit me privately.

"So good to see you, Betty," my mother lied, as she made her move to walk out the door. She leaned in to give her a kiss on the cheek; Gumma moved her lips further to the other side of her head to avoid it. "You too, Lawrence," she traveled to the other side of the bed, her fake sing-songy voice stinging my ears.

When the coast was clear, the tension diminished. Gumma and Da stayed with me until it was dark. Gumma sang to me, Da brought me hot chocolate from the cafeteria. I was even able to drink it without throwing up. Gumma made Radar into a puppet and put on a funny show for me, and the three of us watched Wheel of Fortune, just like we did at home.

Down the Rabbit Hole

While they were with me, I almost forgot I was sick. They always made me feel better.

After nine days on an IV I was finally healthy enough that the doctors could perform the lung tapping procedure. I sat in a chair in my hospital room, my head resting on my bed table as if I were taking a nap at my desk. My father sat across from me, holding my hands and watching. To tap the lungs the surgeon must insert a hollow needle into the back, through the ribcage and "tap" the lung. Fluid is then sucked out and collected in a bag, then sent to the lab to determine the exact nature of the patient's illness. I was not looking forward to this.

"OK, now, this needle is gonna hurt," the surgeon warned me before administering the local anesthesia. "But you won't feel the next one at all, so be brave. It'll be over soon."

I tensed up and held my breath. I squeezed my eyes shut and my father's hands tighter. Then the thick needle pierced my skin, slowly, as if purposefully torturing me. I felt the pressure of liquid being forced into my body and the pain was so intense that I thought they had made a mistake and given me a lethal injection instead. I let out a long, blood curdling scream which ended in sobs. They had gravely undersold the pain.

Down the Rabbit Hole

I heaved and cried into my pillow. Gradually they extracted the needle, and the pain and my tears subsided.

"That was the worst of it," the doctor said.

It better have been, I thought, in my father's condescending tone. As if I could've done anything about it anyway. They could've ripped out my lungs with their bare hands next for all I could do about it.

The doctor proceeded to insert another long, hollowed out needle into my back. I couldn't see what was happening, but according to my father it was "so cool!" Thick, white fluid was extracted from my right lung. It ran down a tube into a bag on the floor next to my chair marked "hazardous." After three minutes they removed the needle and told me I was done. Like a squeamish thrill-seeker I immediately looked to my right and saw the fifty milliliters of milky goo in a bag on the floor. Faintly, I turned away.

"That was awesome!" my man-child of a father exclaimed.

Two days later, I was discharged from the hospital. The test concluded that it had been walking pneumonia caused by the constant inhalation of second-hand smoke.

Down the Rabbit Hole

"Well," my mother began, dismissively. "Sorry, but we're not going to quit."

Down the Rabbit Hole

Chapter 25 — Road Trips

One day while driving in the car my mother instructed me to get her a cigarette out of her purse. She often ordered me to feed her her addictions. I was her bartender when she got too lazy to get up and make herself another drink. Sometimes she'd even tip me a dollar so she could feel classy like a big spender. When she was driving it was up to the passenger to retrieve her cigarettes, gum, glasses. Anything she needed we were to scurry for, as she was busy and could not take her eyes off the road to help herself.

I unzipped her purse, which was seated between us on the armrest, and began to dig through the deep, messy bag in search of the correct brand of cigarette, but I was too slow for her.

"Come on! I'm having a nic fit!" She whined.

She shooed my hands away and grabbed her purse from me, suddenly able to multitask. She promptly found her cancer stick, lit it and inhaled deeply.

Down the Rabbit Hole

I have since learned that a "nicotine fit" is not a real thing. It is an excuse smokers use for their bitchiness when craving a cigarette. It is a non-medical term invented to explain why people get irritable when they can't have what they want when they want it. It is also known as "being a baby," and can be treated with a single dose of shut-the-fuck-up.

My mother smoked two packs a day my entire life. It had probably been only twenty minutes since her last cigarette, so it's unlikely her body was going into a "fit." SHE was throwing a fit, so what she should've said was, "Come on! I'm throwing a fit!" That would've been more accurate.

When driving with Denise, it was also up to the co-pilot to read the map, even if they were too young to do so. My inability to accurately direct us ended up being a good diversion for my mother because it gave her someone to yell at. She had justifiability for her anger if her pre-adolescent passenger got us lost because she was "too stupid" to read a map. We drove halfway cross country numerous times: my mother, sister and me. I dreaded those trips. Nothing stressed my mother out more than moving and she was in an enraged mood the entire trip, every trip.

When I was around nine years old and my sister around four, we drove from Middletown, Connecticut to Chicago, Illinois. This trip was particularly horrible. This was pre-Mapquest so we had to rely on old-fashioned,

Down the Rabbit Hole

oversized, hard-to-read, need-a-magnifying-glass-to-see-your-route maps. I sat up front as I was in charge of reading the map, even though I was only nine and didn't know how to read a fucking map. I was to learn, God damnit, because there were no other options. The stress levels were high.

We left around ten AM and all was smooth until her alcoholic anxiety crept up. Come five PM if my mother didn't have a drink in front of her, everyone would suffer. Her day up until five PM was usually spent preparing for it. This trip interrupted that schedule, and my sister and I would suffer.

Around two PM we stopped for a gas, food and pee break. My sister had a bad habit of lying about not having to go to the bathroom. She was scared to get yelled at for having to go, so when we'd stop my mother would insist that she "just try." Sibby's anxiety made her bladder close up, so even though she tried to, she couldn't pee enough. She'd get some out, but ultimately not properly relieve herself. Like a puppy who's been "trained" by having their nose shoved in their accident, my sister learned that having to pee was bad. We got back in the car and continued on our journey.

Down the Rabbit Hole

Since I could feel my mother approaching a bad mood, I got into the backseat with my sister. We were on the highway for less than ten minutes when Sibby started to squirm in her seat. I knew the pee pee dance all too well.

"Do you have to pee?" I trepidatiously whispered. She started to cry, tears of fear.

"Yes, Punkie please don't tell mommy!"

"What the hell is going on back there?" my mother yelled, warningly.

"Nothing," I answered.

"Do you have to fucking pee, Siobhan?" Denise was also familiar with my sister's shifting.

"Yes, she does," I replied. Because, I mean, what the hell was Sibby gonna do? Hold it for four more hours?

"God fucking damnit, we just fucking stopped!" my mother raged. This was common for both of my parents. They were like pop rocks in coke.

Down the Rabbit Hole

Suddenly exploding, seemingly out of nowhere. My sister was crying real tears now. My mother continued to scream.

"You little piece of shit! You fucking little bitch!" She swerved the car over to the shoulder of the highway, coming to a sudden dead stop.

Guilt engulfed me. This was my fault. If I hadn't said yes she had to pee this wouldn't be happening. I wished more than anything I could take it back. My mother threw open her car door and pulled Sibby out of the backseat.

"Pee right here!" she screamed, pulling down my sister's pants. "You have to pee now? Pee right fucking here on the side of the road!"

Sibby was sobbing hysterically and could barely mutter the words, "I can't!" Cars whizzed by this embarrassing scene. My sister crying, squatting, unable to obey my irate mother who stood over her squeezing her arm. Her bare bottom visible to all who sped by. I'd felt bad before, but I felt absolutely guilt ridden this time. My mother continued to scream at my trembling sister.

"Fucking pee! PEEEEEEEEEE!"

Down the Rabbit Hole

My sister's sobs died down as she closed her eyes and concentrated. A few drops of urine hesitantly fell out of her. This seemed to appease my mother.

"Are you done? Is that all?" My sister nodded. Denise pulled Sibby up to her feet.

"Don't you ever make me do that again! You fucking go when we're at a rest stop." Sibby nodded, relieved for the worst part to be over.

We got back in the car. Again, I sat in back with my sister.

"I'm so sorry, Sibby," I apologized. Her eyes welled up again, but this time with anger.

"Fuck you, Punkie," my four year old sister replied.

Down the Rabbit Hole

Chapter 26 — The World's Best Ten Year Old Mommy

When my sister turned five and began attending school my mother assigned me the task of packing both of our lunches the night before. She couldn't be bothered to get off her lazy ass to construct two PBJ's. That would interrupt her business of tying one on. So making the school lunches became my chore.

I actually enjoyed this task. It gave me an opportunity to act as if I were the perfect mother I wished I had. I took great care in making my sister's lunch. I always cut her sandwich in four "box pieces," just like she liked. I put a piece of fruit and a delicious snack like a hostess cake in her lunchbox. I filled her thermos with hi-c or cool aid… And I wrote her a note.

I was always so envious of kids that had moms that put notes in their lunches. I was jealous of the love they were getting that I was not. I craved that kind of maternal affection. I wished my mother was capable of showing it. Or feeling it. Christ, even faking it. So, since I had the chance now to be the mother I didn't have, I embraced it.

Down the Rabbit Hole

> Dear Sibby, I hope you're having a good day at school. Eat your sandwich first, then your apple, then your snack. Make sure you eat your dessert last. I love you! Xoxo, Punkie

I had undiagnosed OCD. Sometimes it presented itself as anal retentiveness. In my mind, I was going the extra motherly step of instructing my sister on *how* to eat her lunch. This made me a better mother than my sister's classmates moms who just scribbled "love you" on a post-it. I was caring. I provided structure, instruction. Sibby's peers were sure to be jealous of her thoughtful sister.

"Did you get the note I put in your lunch?" I asked her after school.

"Uhhh, yeah." That was not a sufficient response.

"Well, did you eat your sandwich before your dessert?" I pressed.

"I don't know, Punkie. I guess so."

My heart sank. It was like she barely read my note, let alone passed it around the lunchroom to gather praise, like I'd expected. What's that, you say? Expectations are resentments under construction. Well, I didn't know that yet. I was ten, for Christ's sake! Cut me some slack!

Down the Rabbit Hole

Well, hmmf. That didn't go the way I envisioned. See if she ever gets another note in her lunch from me... But I couldn't exercise the stubbornness I felt. The next day I put another note in her lunchbox, this time sans assigned courses. Ultimately, I just liked reminding her that she was loved. My heart was in the right place, even if my desire to control everything was inflated.

"Thank you for the note, Punkie. I love you too," she said to me when she walked in from school that day.

Down the Rabbit Hole

Chapter 27 — Jaba the Head

When I was very young, maybe five years old, I saw a few seconds of *Star Wars*. For years after, I thought Jaba the Hut lived in my head. He was my brain. Or my conscience. Or my God. Or my OCD. He was what I saw when I was thinking. He was me. He was the voice of my thoughts.

He'd give me directions: "circle your thumbs with your pointer fingers three times." Ok. I did it. I didn't know what would happen if I were to disobey. It never came to that. I was a good girl. I just did whatever my brain told me to do.

He'd talk to me as a conscience would. I was scared of him. He was a combination of God and my father. And I couldn't get the image of him talking to me, telling me what to do, out of my head. For years. Every waking moment whenever I had a thought, it was filtered through the fat puppet lips of Jaba.

In a way, it became comforting. Like an imaginary friend. He never told me to hurt myself or anything like that. I mean, sure, he wanted me to do nonsensical things repeatedly for no reason, but what harm was there in that? I was determined to be happy, and if that meant living amicably with a George Lucas creation as my brain, then so be it.

In another way, it was a curse. Why did I have this scary pile of animated poo in *my* head? I was sure other kids didn't have anything like this. And *why* did I have to do things repeatedly? I knew, thanks to my mother's hypochondria, that this was Obsessive Compulsive Disorder, I just didn't know how to stop it.

Jaba began to fade away around fifth grade. We had moved into the house next door to my grandmother's on Bend Lane. I changed school districts, and thus schools. I left Farm Hill and started anew at Bielfield Elementary. I knew a girl in my class, Abigale, through my cousin, so I already had a friend. I had recently lost a bunch of weight due to pneumonia, so I was pretty and confident in my new appearance. No one knew that I'd been unpopular at my old school. I had a clean slate.

I got my first starring roles in the school musical this year. That's right, role*s*. The original musical was titled *Feeling Good*, and its purpose was to teach elementary school children to develop healthy outlooks on life. It was a series of vignettes, each scene addressing an issue kids were dealing with through song.

Down the Rabbit Hole

I got the best part, which was an entire solo scene and song where I sang "Grandpa Play A Song For Me on Your Clarinet." This part was an actor's dream. It had an entire emotional arc. From happily skipping and singing about memories I had of my grandfather playing his clarinet for me, to transitioning into sadness because my grandfather had died. Yeah, it was pretty heavy-handed, but nonetheless it was the best showcase for my vocal and acting talents.

I was also awarded the closing scene, which was a duet about friendship. Ironically the girl who played my "best friend," Susan Gonzales, was my frienemy, and she only got the part because her mother ran drama club. But, since I am such a talented actress I sang, "You Are My Friend," as if she actually was.

After five weeks of rehearsal the rest of Bielfield elementary was forced into the auditorium to watch the masterpiece we'd created. And that day I became the star of the school.

"You have such a good voice," lower classmen whose names I didn't know would say to me at lunch and on the playground.

"Thanks," I'd reply genuinely.

Down the Rabbit Hole

"How long have you been taking voice lessons?" A girl in my class asked me.

"I've never taken voice lessons," I replied.

She was stunned. This gorgeous voice was au natural? Oui.

I was a local star. Two years after *Feeling Good* I was in the video store and the girl working the register asked me if I was the girl who had the solo in *Feeling Good*. I was being recognized! Years later!

"Yes!" I said.

"You have a great voice," she complimented.

Even my mother was floored. "She recognized you from two years ago!" She couldn't believe it.

I had gone from being unpopular and bullied at my old school to respected and envied in my new one. I was developing genuine confidence, and I was happy. For the first time in my life I felt good about myself. With these new attributes, the scary Jaba vanished. I didn't even notice him leaving. Maybe I outgrew him. Maybe he was replaced with confidence. Maybe I got my OCD under control and he just became a part of my tumultuous past. In any event, I didn't miss him. But, because I fear his return, I still won't watch the rest of *Star Wars*.

Down the Rabbit Hole

Chapter 28 — Egging

When I was ten years old my dad's show took us to Washington DC for a few months. We moved into a temporary housing complex, where we were assigned an apartment on the fourteenth floor. This building was nice, compared to some of the other shit-holes we'd been temporarily housed in. There was a front desk in the lobby with a security guard, the front lawn and garden were nicely groomed, and there was an onsite convenience store. It was welcoming. I felt safe walking by myself in this neighborhood. I liked it here.

Our living room window faced the front of the complex where residents parked their cars below. One night my mother, in a rare mischievously fun mood, asked if I wanted to join her in throwing eggs out of the window at the cars. Did I ever! Fun-drunk mom was better than angry-drunk mom, so I took the money she gave me, went downstairs to the in-house convenience store and bought a dozen eggs. Eager anticipation filled me as I rode the elevator back up to the fourteenth floor. A chance to bond with mom! How scarce these opportunities were. Maybe I'd make her laugh and she'd realize what a great kid I was. Perhaps this was the start of a new chapter in our relationship: the close years. The time when we would become best friends, like the mothers and daughters I read about in my young adult novels. I longed for a relationship like that. I entered our apartment with a smile on my face.

The next ten minutes were some of the best mother daughter time we'd ever had. Side by side we sat at the window, lining up our aims.

"One, two, three, go!" we said in unison, before letting our eggs fly.

Laughing after we released our ammunition, we'd fall to the floor, ducking out of sight of anyone who might be wandering below. After a few seconds passed, and our giggles subsided, we'd creep back up to peek out of our large bay window to see where we'd hit. The dozen eggs were gone too fast, but we were having too much fun to stop, so my new best friend gave me another five dollar bill from her purse and I scurried back down to the lobby to get twelve more eggs.

But by the time I made it back to our makeshift home my mother's mood had changed to annoyance. She joined me in throwing a few more rounds out of obligation, but her happy-go-lucky attitude had given way to the condescending anger I was most familiar with. She had gotten bored with our activity and wanted to be alone. Taking her childish defiance as my cue, I silently put the rest of the carton into the fridge and went into my room to give her her space.

Down the Rabbit Hole

A half hour later there was a knock on our door. A policeman and an apartment security guard stood authoritatively. Unaware of who he was dealing with, the police officer stated that they'd gotten reports of people throwing eggs out of their window. My mother, never the most convincing actress, lied.

"No! I don't know anything about it! Kate!" She called me out of hiding. "Were you throwing eggs out the window?!"

Dumbfounded, caught off guard and scared, I lied.

"No."

I shouldn't have been surprised that she tried to save herself while throwing me under the bus, but I was a little hurt. The two authority figures seemed unconvinced and uninterested. Their job here was to scare us, and that was done. They left.

Immediately my mother turned into the rage monster and the real punishment began.

Down the Rabbit Hole

"You stupid little bitch!" She punched-slapped me into the wall. "You stupid fucking cunt! You're gonna get us evicted!"

She continued to hit as I huddled into a ball to try and protect myself.

"If you do I swear to God I will leave you on the side of the road! I'll drive you into the fucking ghetto and leave you there where you'll be raped and murdered!"

How little she knows, I felt sorry for myself. *That sounds like heaven compared to this.*

Finally she ran out of physical energy and disgustedly spat. "Get out of my sight!"

Oh, how I loved those words! They were permission to leave. They always came, once she could hit no more. Once she got bored and could think up no new insults, she'd dismiss me with those words. I crawled into my room and cried myself to sleep.

The following day I feared what was to come. Denise wasn't talking to me, but I could see the wheels of anger turning in her head. Her silence was terrifying. It meant she was planning, plotting her explosion.

Down the Rabbit Hole

We dropped my father off at the theatre. I silently prayed he would spontaneously invite me to spend the day with him at work. No such luck. We drove a few blocks, out of the safe zone, in silence. Then my mother spun around to me in the backseat. She was irate.

"How dare you pull a prank like that!" She falsely accused me of initiating the previous night's events. "You could've gotten us evicted!" she repeated, and began to multi task swat-punching me while driving.

My sister sat next to me in the backseat, unsure of what to do besides continue to be traumatized. She didn't know what was going on, as she had been asleep for the egg-tossing event and its subsequent ordeals. She said nothing as Denise continued to yell and hit. I cried and attempted to curl up in a ball to avoid her hand. Finally, suddenly, she swerved over to the side of the road.

"Get out! Get the fuck out of my car!" She pushed and pushed me into the door until I opened it and fell out onto the curb.

With the back door still open, she sped off. I stood up quickly, embarrassed, and tried to erase the physical evidence of the previous scene. Wiping my eyes and straightening my clothes, I looked around. I had no

Down the Rabbit Hole

idea where I was. An empty bus stop was in front of me, a tall building across the street. There were no street signs. I stood and wondered what to do next. *I should never go back,* I fantasized. *This could be my chance to start a new life for myself. I can go live in an abandoned building, like they did in No Place Like Home. I can fend for myself. I'll be ok... and if I die maybe Denise will realize what a terrible mother she is,* my inner voice turned maudlin. *She'll be sorry for leaving me in the middle of nowhere if I do get raped and murdered.* Honestly, it seemed a better option than going home.

"Are you lost?" An old woman interrupted my rabbit holing.

"Yes, my mom left me." I was never shy about telling people the truth.

"Oohh," she cooed sympathetically. "Do you need to use the phone?"

She took me by the arm and led me across the street to the tall apartment building, a senior housing complex. I used the phone in the lobby to call my dad at work, while this nice woman sat with me. I fantasized that she adopted me, like the old man in *Punky Brewster*. But the reality was she was sending me back to the wicked birth parents.

Down the Rabbit Hole

My dad sighed with annoyance, but spoke compassionately, "Take a cab to the theatre, Punkie," he instructed.

I obeyed. Triggered and feeling alone, I stayed with him all night as he worked. My sadness dissipated as I watched *Les Miz* from his flying post in the wings. I imagined I were Little Cosette, and took comfort in the faith that someday Val Jean would come rescue me.

When the show ended my father and I went home. With hours of traveling down the rabbit hole inside *his* head, he'd had time to stir up some rage. He bounded through the door and threw my mother to the ground.

"You left your daughter on the side of the road?! You stupid fucking cunt!"

This gave my mother the opportunity to play her favorite role: victim.

"Eddie, no!" She over reacted. "Don't beat me! Don't beat me!"

He did not listen. He pulled her up by her hair and threw her into the wall. I stood smiling, suddenly pulled out of my triggered state. *How you like me now, bitch?* I thought at her. If I'd had a microphone I would've dropped it. Everything was better now. I had been avenged. At least temporarily, I had won.

Down the Rabbit Hole

Chapter 29 — Lessons

I've known that I want to be an actress since I was a little girl. Watching my dad's shows from his post in the wings, I'd marvel at the performers and say, "I wanna do that when I grow up."

"You have to learn how to play an instrument," my pessimistic mother, in a drunken stupor, informed me. "All of those actors are triple threats. They can sing, dance, act *and* play an instrument." I silently corrected her math skills. Her attempt to dissuade me did the opposite.

"Can I take piano lessons?" little seven year old me asked meekly.

"No, they're too expensive," my mother replied automatically.

Well, she must've felt bad or simply remembered my request, when she found an old used piano for cheap on sale nearby. My father bought it and my mother found Ms. Krause, a retired music teacher, to come to the house for private lessons for one hour a week at ten dollars an hour. I was ecstatic!

Down the Rabbit Hole

The first week she taught me finger placement and how to move my hands across the keys. We did very little actual hitting of keys. I was bummed because I'd hoped to be playing "Fur Elise" by the end of my first hour, but she explained that learning an instrument takes time and first things were first. I had to learn the basics before I could play. I understood that. But my mother, as impatient as always, did not.

"Are you sure you want to continue taking piano lessons?" she neurotically inquired after just one lesson, hoping I'd say no to recoup those ten dollars a week for her cocaine fund.

"Yes, I'm sure," I said, not giving in.

The following week Ms. Krause returned and we went over the fingering from the week before. After a half hour of review, we moved onto reading music. She taught me basic note reading using the mnemonic device Every Good Boy Does Fine, as well as the meaning of symbols such as clefs. I enjoyed this lesson. I was learning something and I looked forward to learning more.

But when Ms. Krause left my mother, noticing that we'd still not played any Bach, impatiently asked again: "Are you sure you like piano? It *is* ten dollars an hour..."

Down the Rabbit Hole

"I'm sure," I repeated. It was the truth.

The next week's lesson followed suit. Half an hour of review, then I got to play. Only a few notes, only with my right hand, but it was an accomplishment to see a note on the page and be able to find the correct key. Sure, I hit the wrong key a few times. Sure, I had to stop and ask questions. But slowly I was learning... very slowly... too slowly if you're my mother. Nothing was ever fast enough for her.

When Ms. Krause left that afternoon my mother sat down next to me on the piano bench for a heart to heart.

"Punkie, if you don't like piano you don't have to continue taking lessons. It *is* ten dollars an hour, so if you don't really love it..."

I felt like a failure as I considered quitting, and I felt guilty at the thought of continuing. Perhaps it was the fact that my mother chose to level with me, to sit with me as if we were equals. Or maybe it was because feeling guilty that she was spending money on me simply outweighed feeling like a failure for quitting. Or perhaps I knew eventually the piano would be taken away from me regardless and this may be the last chance I had to quit "on my own terms," but I gave in.

Down the Rabbit Hole

"No, Mom" I answered her. "I don't love it." That was all she needed to hear.

"Ok," she said, getting up. "I'll call Ms. Krause and cancel... it's ok, Punkie. There will be other things."

I felt horrible because I didn't want to quit. But I'd let my mother passive-aggressively bully me into it. It was too late to change my mind, to tell her I wanted to continue. Now she had the power and would say no, the decision had been made. I wanted to cry.

The following year I decided I wanted to take dance lessons. A bunch of girls at Farm Hill took classes at Miss Beth's and they loved it. They were skinny and I was chubby, so I thought dance would help me lose weight and make friends. Convincing my parents to enroll me was harder than convincing them to let me take piano.

"You don't have the body for dance," my mother said. "Those girls are tiny and athletic. You'll be the biggest girl in your class."

After much debate they finally let me enroll in ballet which met once a week. And she was right. I was the biggest girl in this beginners class because I was also the oldest. But I also proved to be the fastest learner, so I was given a front and center spot in our dance routine, which we'd perform at our year-end recital.

Miss Beth's assistant came into class one day to measure us for costumes.

"You're gonna be an awfully big ballerina," she shamed me.

I felt awful. I was constantly chastised for my weight by my peers, so it hurt even more to be criticized by this old woman. It was as if she was confirming that my bullies were right and I was wrong. When I got home from class that night, I told my dad.

"The costume lady said I am gonna be a big ballerina."

My father, who struggled with his own weight, was upset by this.

"Don't listen to her, Punkie," he soothed, putting his arm around me and hugging me.

I tried to go on a diet.

Down the Rabbit Hole

"You've just got to cut out desserts," my mother helped.

I vowed that I would stop eating sweets and would lose so much weight by show time that they'd have to pin my costume on me to make it stay up. But by nighttime I craved dessert so bad that I changed my mind.

"One dessert a day should be fine," I rationalized, and my vodka-buzzed mother agreed.

I had a boring bowl of vanilla ice cream with no toppings, thinking that I was upholding my diet because I didn't enjoy it.

Next week in class we ran our dance.

"Watch Kate if you get lost," I heard Miss Chelsea tell the girls in the second row.

I felt a momentary surge of confidence. My teacher was telling everyone to watch me because I knew the dance! I never messed up! I was the best in the class! To hell with my mother who said that I'd never be a good dancer! I was proving her wrong!

Down the Rabbit Hole

But as soon as the music started all of the steps left my head. My confident bubble burst and I panicked. I looked in the mirror to follow everyone else, but they were all looking at me. Miss Chelsea stopped the music and came up to me.

"Kate," she whispered in a good-natured whine, "what happened? I told everyone to watch you for the steps." Her easygoing tone soothed me and I relaxed.

"I know, I'm sorry. I got it now." She started the music from the top and I returned as the group leader.

The following year I told my parents I wanted to take jazz.

"Jesus Christ," my mother huffed, "money doesn't grow on trees."

But eventually she relented and allowed me to sign up. She dropped me off out front with a check for the month's lessons, then sped off home to get some drinking in before she had to pick me up an hour later. I walked inside and surveyed the waiting room. It was full of mothers helping their kids get ready for class. Tying their hair in buns, and lacing up their shoes. Talking to the teachers and to each other. I longed for a mother like that. One who stayed the hour, watching the class from the window in the lobby. Or one who brought her crochet kit to occupy herself quietly until class let out. I was the only little girl waiting in line to pay. When I got to the window Miss Beth gave me a strange look.

"You're by yourself?" she asked.

"Yeah. My mom dropped me off." I tried to shrug it off, make it sound like it was no big deal to me, but it was. It was lonely.

This routine continued for two months: Denise dropping me off at six PM then speeding off for an hour of power drinking before resentfully picking me back up at seven. Eventually, she made me quit dance, too.

"I can't keep dropping you off and picking you up like this. I'm not a taxi service. Plus I have bad night vision."

A lump formed in my throat. *No, that's blurred vision,* I thought. *It happens when you drink too much.* But I knew I was powerless over this decision. The call had been made and arguing with her would only piss her off. I retreated to my room so she wouldn't see me cry.

Down the Rabbit Hole

I was nowhere near giving up on my dream of becoming an actress, so the following year I tried again. I asked to take voice lessons and my parents said yes.

Once a week I stayed after school and practiced with a vocal coach from the Hartt school of music. She taught me how to properly warm up my voice before singing. We did scales and breathing exercises. Then she introduced me to Italian sonatas. To be honest, I found the lessons and the sonatas boring, but I never wanted to quit. I understood that I had to get through the boring stuff before I got to *Les Miz*, so I never spoke ill of the process to my parents. I was careful to only say how much I loved voice lessons. I was smart enough to know not to give them any reason to pull the rug out from under me.

But after a few months they did anyway. With the same excuses. "It's too expensive," "Mom can't come pick you up," "It's too late," even though these lessons were directly after school and done by 4:30, "You're ungrateful," "You don't appreciate it." I wasn't surprised. I was expecting this. I had planned on being forced to quit, so I preemptively built a wall up around my feelings so they wouldn't get hurt. When my mother revealed to me that these lessons were over now too, with a gleam of sick enjoyment in her eyes, I was numb. I felt nothing. And I felt like I won. Finally. I felt powerful.

Chapter 30 — Gumma's Back Porch

My mother was a nightly blackout drinker, but she never picked up before five PM. It was one of the ways she bargained with her disease.

She'd sit at the dining room table in front of the TV, chain smoking and judging everyone from nightly news anchors to JR Ewing. Occasionally she'd drunk dial Lucky and Brandy Lewis in Louisiana: "friends" she'd met through the *Les Miz* tour. I'd hear her attempting to gossip with Brandy about their kids. She'd pry into their lives, asking questions you'd only ask your closest friends.

"Is Mason having sex yet?" The drink had made her ballsy.

I would hear Brandy on the other end of the line, uncomfortably looking for a graceful exit. Eventually they stopped answering when she called. My pathetic, sick mother. She just didn't want to be drunk alone.

I was eleven years old and in sixth grade. We were living in Connecticut, next door to Gumma, while my dad worked on a show in New York City. He commuted into the city every day, leaving for work at two in the afternoon. Most days I didn't see him. I was playing Dorothy in my middle school's production of *The Wizard of Oz*, and had to stay after school every day for rehearsal. This, of course, pissed my mother off, because it cut into her drinking time. Having to pick me up at six meant she had to stay sober enough to drive across town to Kegwin and back until six. She resented me deeply for this inconvenience, but for some reason, I'm guessing to do with my dad, she had not yet made me quit this show.

One night, around eleven PM, after begrudgingly picking me up and resuming her post at the dining room table she called me.

"KATE!"

I had retreated to my room and closed the door to escape her wrath, so she made sure her booming voice would penetrate the walls that separated us. It was more of a scream than a call. As if she was on fire and time was of the essence. I hurriedly ran downstairs, for you were to *go* to my parents when they beckoned. To simply answer, "what?" was a sign of disrespect and would result in a beating.

I entered the dining room and she put the TV on mute. *Oh God,* I thought, *this roast requires her undivided attention.*

"Sit," she ordered.

Down the Rabbit Hole

She was pissed. I had done nothing to motivate her bad mood, except attempt to live a normal pre-adolescent life, but that was enough to enrage her. I sat, and immediately she grabbed the underside of my chair and pulled it too close to her. Grabbing my face, she put her nose to mine.

"You'll never be a real actress, you're too fat!" she spat, throwing my face away from hers in disgust.

My eyes welled up with tears against my will. *God damnit! Fuck her!* I thought. I was getting too old for this shit. I was almost as big as her now, but still she abused me like I was a tiny dog. She was pathetic, sitting there, night after night, chain smoking and drinking alone. The more she drank, the more she badmouthed and berated people on TV, my father, my grandmother, her co-workers. Everyone was a victim to her drunken name calling. It was sick, pitiful and desperate.

She picked up a cigarette and lit in.

"You have no other talents," she continued matter-of-factly. "These people you see in your dad's shows have been doing it their whole lives. They're in the business before they're out of diapers."

Down the Rabbit Hole

She had clearly thought this through.

"Well, I can sing..." I began to meekly defend myself, but she promptly dismissed it.

"Yeah, yeah, you can sing. These people have been professionally trained their whole lives!"

I quashed my desire to bring up the fact that I'd been forced to give up voice and dance lessons because it interfered with her boozing, but I couldn't get a thought in edgewise.

"Plus you're too fat! No one's gonna hire you, you're fat!" she seethed.

It was hard to remain strong when she was so determined to beat me down. There was no winning this. There never was. I just prayed she'd fizzle and not get a second wind.

But, of course, she did. She grabbed my chair again and pulled it even closer toward hers.

Down the Rabbit Hole

"YOU HAVE NO TALENTS!" she screamed in my face, as if volume would get her insults through my thick skull.

I was terrified of her. She was unpredictable when she was this wound up. All I knew how to do was remain silent and pray. *Please God, get me out of this*, I begged my higher power, who was kind and loving. She grabbed my face again and spat in it. I shook myself free from her grasp and wiped her saliva from my face. But she was full of resentful energy. Getting up out of her chair, she pushed me off mine. I fell backwards onto the floor. Then she climbed on top of me.

"YOU'RE NOTHING!" she vociferously screamed. I struggled under her, but she grabbed me by the hair and pulled my head back. I cried even harder.

"Please stop!" I pleaded, but she liked it when I begged. It gave her power. She snorted condescendingly. She grabbed my face in her hands and squeezed.

"You're nothing. And you'll never be anything." She had to have the last word. Then, in a grand finale, she threw my face to the side, stepped over me and kicked me.

Down the Rabbit Hole

Finally out from under her, I scurried up off the floor and ran out the front door. I was terrified she'd follow me, but she didn't. She'd accomplished her goal of making me feel like shit; she needed nothing more from me that evening. I ran next door to the safety of my Gumma's. The lights in her kitchen were dimmed, which meant she'd gone upstairs for the evening. I rang the temperamental doorbell, which only worked when it felt like it, and screamed, "GUMMA!" repeatedly. I banged and banged on the door and rang and rang the doorbell and screamed and screamed her name, but nothing. I looked over my shoulder, at the house to my left, fearing my mother were a monster walking slowly towards me, but of course she was not. She was too lazy to leave the house, no matter how mad she was. Gumma still did not answer. She couldn't hear the doorbell or my cries... I could not go home. I'd have to stay outside tonight.

I often played house on this back porch. There were two chairs immediately when you walked up the three stairs. Between them was a small wooden folding table with a plant on it. I'd make believe that this was my living room. To the right was a closet where my grandmother hung the winter coats that were too bulky to keep inside. To the left of the back door was another, larger plastic porch chair. I'd make that my bedroom. Then, an outdoor table with two chairs on either side of it. That was my dining room. Next to the table was an outdoor grill: my kitchen. The porch floor was wall-to-wall green fake grass carpet. On the wall, the side of the house, was a portrait of a sad clown from the circus my grandparents had met in. Plants and wind chimes hung on every open hook. I loved this porch. I'd pretend it was my house tonight. I felt a sense of calm come over me. Of peace. Of freedom.

I pushed two chairs together to make my bed. I opened the closet and used three winter coats to make bedding. I put on a large coat to keep me warm, and used another as a blanket.

Attempting to get comfortable, I began to worry. We lived across the street from Connecticut Valley Hospital, a psychiatric institution. Yeah, seriously. As if this story couldn't get any more unbelievable. I remembered the stories my grandmother had told me about escaped patients who wandered onto their property.

The first time was when my father was a little boy. They had a dog, Ike, and one night while they were all in the living room watching TV, he wouldn't stop barking. My grandmother finally let him out and he chased down two men who were hiding in the shadows looking into the living room window.

The second time my grandfather went out to put the car in the garage and found a man sitting behind the steering wheel.

Down the Rabbit Hole

I wondered why they never lit their backyard better after these incidents, although lighting four acres would probably be pretty expensive. At night it was so dark you couldn't even see right in front of you. It was possible there were people hiding in the shadows right now, only a few feet from me...

Everything is going to be ok, I told myself. Or perhaps God told me. I laid in my makeshift bed and retreated into my thoughts. *What have I done to deserve such a terrible mother?* I asked God. *It will all be worth it someday,* I heard him answer. I felt taken care of. Don't get me wrong, I felt scared, lonely, sad, helpless and stuck too. But I felt a strong sense that ultimately I'd be ok. Eventually this will all pay off. I will be a stronger person because of incidents like these. I will overcome.

Finally, I drifted off to sleep. After two hours or so I woke up frozen and stiff. The sun hadn't risen completely. The backyard was heavy with damp fog. I opened my eyes. Standing under my swing set, only thirty or so feet from me were two beautiful deer: a mother and a fawn. They looked at me, aware I had woken up. I did not move. I didn't want to scare them and I didn't want them to leave. They were majestic and I was so grateful for their presence. I'd never seen the backyard like this. It was so misty I couldn't see beyond my swing set. And I'd never seen a deer so close to the house before. I wanted this moment to last. And just like that, they turned and ran away. Back to the woods in the way way back yard where they had come from. I envied their freedom, to come and go as they pleased. I wished I could've been as free as them.

Just then Gumma opened the back door.

"For heaven's sake, what are you doing out here?" she asked, surprised to see me camping on her back porch.

"My mother beat me last night, and I had to run out of there," I began to explain, my eyes welling up with tears as I relived the trauma from the night before.

I got up as I spoke, and began moving the chairs back to their spots.

"Leave it, leave it! Come inside!" Gumma instructed me. She held the door open and I fell into her arms.

"Now, now. No crying! When you cry, you make me cry," she said, wiping my tears away.

Down the Rabbit Hole

I hugged her and she cradled me, abolishing my fears and assuring me that everything was ok now.

"I banged on the door and rang and rang the doorbell," I explained to my elderly grandmother, "but you couldn't hear."

"If that ever happens again, you go to the *front* door and bang as hard as you can," she instructed. "I'll hear that," she assured me.

She led me upstairs and tucked me into her bed, where I slept for half the day.

I awoke that afternoon to the telephone ringing. It was my mother.

"Kate, come home," she ordered.

She did not sound sorry. I didn't want to go, but I had no choice. Slowly, in a triggered state, I hugged my grandmother goodbye, and went back next door to the dungeon of terror I called home. My mother ignored me when I entered. Scared, alone, and far down the rabbit hole, I retreated to my room, shutting the door behind me.

Chapter 31 — Confiding in the Shower

My father's untreated mind rabbit holed differently than mine. Once he starts thinking, he free falls right down into an abyss of *I'm right, everyone else is wrong, here is why.* Justify, justify, justify. Defend, defend, defend. *There is only one side to this story, only one correct course of action, and that is mine.* His mind will beat that dead horse, convincing itself that it is right, repeating its arguments with different imaginary audiences, who all agree, because that is the only conclusion his narrow mind will allow. Nothing else exists. It is complete self obsession.

The morning after a domestic dispute I overheard my father talking to himself in the shower.

"Just shut the fuck up," he was saying over and over again, as if he were still trying to control my mother in whatever their dispute was the night before. "Just shut up," he said, his intonation suggesting that if she had, he wouldn't have been forced to explode on her.

I could hear his lonely smile. He was completely immersed in himself, in his conclusion that he was right. He had convinced himself, yet again, that his outburst was one hundred percent Denise's fault. He was blameless. If only she'd listened. I mean, how hard is it to just shut the fuck up? Didn't she see that if she just behaved the way he thought she should behave, the previous evening could've culminated in matrimonial bliss? It wasn't my father who had an anger problem; it was my mother who had a behavioral problem. *He* was the reasonable one.

When I accidentally overheard this monologuing rant my immediate reaction was embarrassment. *Oh! That's not something I'm supposed to hear!* Fear quickly followed. *I'd better get out of here before Dad hears and turns his anger on me.* But then a sneaking sense of familiarity crept in. I could identify with his thought process. I too had had long cerebral showers where I traveled into the lonely depths of my mind, convincing myself that I had all the right answers and if only everyone else could see what was in my mind they'd find the keys to success and happiness and peace and harmony. But I'd never thought of it that way - until now. I mean, I'd never overheard someone else doing it and so I'd never even thought about the fact that I engaged in it at all. All the time. Suddenly there was this mirror that I was too embarrassed to look into. Wait... was I crazy? Because my father sounded crazy. Was I so self-obsessed that I believed I had all the right answers? Because he sure seemed to think he did, too...

Down the Rabbit Hole

Why did he sound so defensive? Because he was obsessed with being right, but deep down felt guilty for the way he'd acted. Since he wasn't willing to consciously admit any responsibility, he had to rant about it to anyone in his head who would listen. There were a lot of people in his mind to convince today, to relay his side of the story too. He had friends up there who agreed that he had been one hundred percent right the night before when he exploded in a rage, throwing my mother and her chair to the ground. There was also the tired police officer who showed up at three AM mulling around in my father's brain. He seemed to need a little extra convincing. There were the mutual friends who Denise would get to first to sweep back onto his side. Should be easy. I mean, *he* was the reasonable one here.

I would learn later in life that the deep, dark, lonely rabbit hole of our mind is also known as a triggered state. It is a feeling of complete powerlessness that the mind cannot handle, so it reassures you that you're not wrong or lonely or afraid. It tells you that you're right and everyone else is wrong. When all else fails, it's a coping mechanism. If only *they* would act the way *we* thought they should, the world would be a better place. I mean, come on, how hard is it?

So, it was ultimately fear that I heard that day. Disguised as reason. Fronting as anger, frustration and power. But very clearly, when you strip away the bullshit, fear. My father, and subsequently I, were deathly afraid of being humble.

I would also learn later in life that humility isn't as hard as it seems. In fact, it's quite easy and so much simpler than repeatedly defending oneself into a lonely corner. It is our defensiveness that separates us from others. When we learn to let that strategy go, we find that people actually like us more. Even more importantly, we come to like ourselves more. But on this sad morning my father was miles away from humble. If only he'd realized that he was but one simple step from the peace he craved.

He would never swallow that humble pill. His anger would continue to fester and grow and force its way out in abusive fits of violent rage. He would submerse himself in Rush Limbaugh, brainwashing himself daily with authoritarian talk radio. His hero was another lonely man who could also do no wrong. What I remember most about the Rush Limbaugh show, which played 24/7 on all electronic devices in every room in our home, was the dead air. The scary moments where Rush let the audience absorb the brilliance he'd just spouted. In fact, I never really remember what Rush said. I only recall being scared that if I didn't agree with him, he'd yell at me until I did. He was my father. Scary, combative and, without fail, always right.

Down the Rabbit Hole

Chapter 32 — Group

Before entering sixth grade, students were given an anonymous questionnaire. Did we suspect our parents were using drugs? Had we ever seen them do drugs? What drugs? How often? Did they hit us? Leave us unattended? How often? Did they drink? How often?

Yup, that's right. There were enough deadbeat, strung out, neglectful parents in my hometown to warrant a survey that turned their kids into little narcs. But I was happy to answer these questions honestly because, as usual, I thought they'd lead to me being removed from my home by child protective services.

The "anonymous" part was bullshit, as we were asked to put the first three letters of our last name and our birthdate on the top. I guess the teacher's association thought fifth graders were too naive to know what anonymous meant, but I had heard of Alcoholics Anonymous, so I didn't fall for the guise of secrecy. Plus, I *wanted* the adults in my school to know what I was going through on a daily basis at home. How could they help me if they didn't know?

Down the Rabbit Hole

Elementary school in Middletown, Connecticut was first through fifth grade. There were seven elementary schools in Middletown, but there was only one sixth grade: Kegwin. Twelve year olds who'd never met were forced to interface from seven to three Monday through Friday at this new school. Perhaps it would help us develop some social skills.

When the sixth grade started, students were informed that some of us would be attending "group." "Group" was code for group therapy. For one period per week flagged students were allowed to skip class, and attend talk sessions with other students and a social worker. Groups were categorized by children of addicts, children of alcoholics, and abused children. There were approximately six groups total, four to ten students in each. Due to my extremely shitty circumstances I was a member of not one, but two, groups. So for two hours per week I got to talk about my horrible home life with people who were going through the same thing - and I loved it. I felt safe to speak the truth in group and not be judged. I felt camaraderie and support. I felt relief and hope. I stopped feeling so alone. I started making real friends, not just with people in my groups, but with other students as well. I opened up. I became a little more whole.

I'd share about the worst things that happened at home. No matter how embarrassing the situation was, I shared it. And I got the condolences and support I was looking for from my peers. They became puppy-dog eyed and hung their heads in sympathy when I spoke. They felt for me, and I appreciated it. But theirs was not the sympathy I needed in order to get what I wanted most.

My social workers called the Department of Child and Family Services numerous times on my behalf. I straight-up requested to be placed in foster care. Anything would be better than going home every night. But no matter how hard I pleaded, my wish was never granted.

"Do you realize you'll be taken out of your home forever?" my vice principal asked me as I sat in her office in tears while my social worker called DCF yet again.

"Yes! That's what I want!"

No matter how adamant I was, it seemed no adult believed I knew how serious being put into foster care was. But I understood enough. It seemed *they* didn't understand how unlivable my situation at home was. I was not only prepared for a drastic change, I was begging for it.

Once a DCF employee came to our house. Once. After my social worker called dozens of times. Finally, if only just to stop us from calling, she made an appearance. The woman interviewed me and my mom separately. Surprisingly Denise was her usual annoyed self. She didn't even try to put on a happy facade. She'd have been glad to get rid of me, so she risked being as honest as possible without getting charged with a felony, and let the chips fall where they may.

I eavesdropped on their conversation. Yes, she hit me occasionally. I deserved it. No, she wasn't abusive, she was a disciplinarian. There was a difference. Yes, she drank at night, but she wasn't an alcoholic. No, she never used drugs.

"I've seen their white powder," I told Ms. DCF. "I think it's crack or cocaine." Thanks DARE program. "She gets so drunk every night she doesn't even remember what she's done the next day. She beats me all the time for no reason."

After our brief questioning Ms. DCF walked through our house making notes and then left. We never heard from her again. My social worker called repeatedly to follow up, but she never returned our calls.

Perhaps she'd assessed that my situation just wasn't bad enough to take me out of. It'd have been nice to know that. She'd have been wrong, but at least she could say she was doing her job and giving us an answer,

Down the Rabbit Hole

albeit one we didn't like. I felt powerless and hopeless. I was angry at the system. What was it there for if not to help people in my exact situation?

The only thing I could think of was that DCF was underfunded, so it was simply impossible to help all those who needed it. My family and I are White, middle class, and my father made a good living on paper. Middletown was full of poverty. There were two sets of housing projects. Many kids in my school had only one parent. Many were on welfare and food stamps. There was a reason Middletown kids were given that "anonymous" questionnaire and not Fairfield kids. Middletown wasn't the nice part of Connecticut. Perhaps if I'd lived in Avon, DCF would've found it fit to place me in a foster home. But I guess Middletown just had too many deadbeat parents to deal with every one of their unwanted spawn.

Thankfully, gradually, I was learning how to cope on my own. I was meeting and sharing with peers in similar situations and that helped alleviate some of my pain. If my circumstances couldn't be improved, maybe my outlook could.

Chapter 33 — *Fiddler on the Roof*

Fresh off the heels of my show-stopping performance as Dorothy in *The Wizard of Oz,* I was cast in the East Hartford dinner theatre production of *Fiddler on the Roof.* I played Shprintz, the second to last daughter. I was on a roll. I was determined to never be out of work and to consistently move up in the industry, so this production fit nicely into my plan. Unfortunately, it did not fit so nicely into my mother's plans, which were to get hammered every night.

Rehearsals were in an old lounge in the lobby of a hotel in East Hartford four nights a week from six to ten PM. For the first few rehearsals my mother drove us there enthusiastically. She must've challenged herself to stop drinking because she actually sat and watched, attentively, sans cocktail.

"I saw the director's eyebrows go up when he heard you sing," she gossiped. "He's obviously impressed with your voice."

For the first few days my mother was my fan. But by the third night she let her restlessness get ahold of her.

Down the Rabbit Hole

"I'll be back to get you after rehearsal," she said, and went off to the hotel bar.

At ten PM I exited the lounge and tentatively began walking towards the bar, afraid of who'd replaced my sober mother. Sitting alone at a table, angrily smoking and finishing another vodka/tonic, sat my drunk mom. Belligerence, defiance and condescension colored her face, along with all the broken blood vessels.

"Jesus Christ! You've been in there for fucking ever!" she spat.

"You know rehearsal goes until ten," I answered softly.

"I'm not fucking driving you to this shit anymore. You wanna stay in the show, find your own way there and back."

I should've seen this coming. But I'd naively hoped that once I was under contract she couldn't back out. I thought I'd be protected from my mother's alcoholism by this professional theatre company. But no such luck. She bolted out of the bar and into the cold parking lot. I had to run to keep up with her. She would've left me there, she was so angry drunk. I stayed silent, trying to figure out how I could get rides to and from East Hartford four nights a week. I was sure my grandmother would be good

Down the Rabbit Hole

for one night, even though she was old and not a very good driver. Maybe there was someone else who lived in Middletown that I could ask for rides another night? I could take a cab the rest of the time. It'd take all of my allowance and babysitting money that I'd saved, but maybe...

"You're going to have to drop out of the show," my mother announced.

"No!" I exclaimed. "I can ask Gumma for a ride!"

"You're not asking your eighty-year old grandmother to drive you to East Hartford at night!" she shouted.

But what she meant was, *You're not telling your grandmother I can't take you because it cuts into my drinking time.*

"I can take a cab!" I pleaded.

"I'm not paying a cab to take you to and from East Hartford four nights a week!"

"I'll pay for it!"

"You can't afford it! Plus, you'll get raped and murdered."

Down the Rabbit Hole

"Please," I pleaded, holding back tears. "Please just keep taking me!"

"NO!" she screamed.

I shut up so she didn't silence me with her fists.

The next day I tried to reason with my father.

"I don't know what you want me to do about it, I've gotta work," he shrugged.

"Just tell her to take me. Can't you make her take me?" I was trying not to cry.

"She doesn't have to do anything," he began defiantly. Then he softened, "I'm sorry, Punkie, but there will be other plays."

My mother made me make the call to the Starlight Production office myself, but she had told me what to say so as to not burn this bridge. This was how you resign while maintaining your professional reputation, according to her. So with a script written by her on an index card, I left a message.

Down the Rabbit Hole

"I'm so sorry, but I have to withdraw from the Starlight dinner theatre's production of *Fiddler on the Roof* due to scheduling conflicts with another role. I sincerely apologize for any inconvenience this may cause. Thank you so much for this opportunity. Please keep me in mind for future productions."

My heart broke with the finality of that message. But still I hung onto a small shred of hope that maybe my mother would have a change of heart. Or maybe the director would call and beg her to let me participate. The show just couldn't go on without me! There was something in me that would not let me fully accept that the show *would* go on without me. It was just too difficult, too painful to accept... But my mother did not change her mind. And no one from the production called me. And life went on. And it was ok. There were other roles. I was able to make it all the way to many closing nights.

Chapter 34 — Our Sociopathic Father and our Suicidal Dog

We got Schuylar, a miniature dachshund puppy, when I was eleven years old. I had wanted a dog for awhile and my parents eventually caved. I longed for a loyal companion to snuggle up to when I was feeling alone, and I vowed to become the best doggie mommy in the whole wide world. I'd have him catching a frisbee like that dog in *Flight of the Navigator* in no time.

On his first night in his new home, I made Schuylar a bed out of a plastic stacker tray and some old bankies. When I determined it was bedtime for my new baby, I tucked him in and told him to stay. He laid cozily in place while I snapped a picture, then promptly untucked himself and peed right next to his new bed.

Training a dog is hard when you don't know how to train a dog. My parents were too cheap to spring for obedience school, and too self-absorbed to walk Schuylar, so they decided to paper train him using the best method they knew: their own sense. They lined the floor in our mud room with newspaper and expected him to know that he was supposed to relieve himself there. When he had an accident on the floor they stuck his nose in it, spanked him, then shook Tabasco sauce in his face. Oddly enough this sure-fire tactic didn't work. Schuylar never became fully house trained. Instead he became riddled with anxiety. He'd use the papers half the time; the other half he'd have accidents all over the house.

In fact, he was so randomly afraid of people that he suffered incontinence if they even looked at him. My friend Erica and I had a running joke that when she came over she was not to make eye contact with my pup. For some reason, although she never abused him, she scared him so much that he'd pee at the sight of her.

That fall my father raked the leaves in the backyard into huge piles and introduced an idea that he said would be "fun."

"Punkie, watch this," he said, throwing Schuylar into a pile of maple leaves.

Because I didn't know any better and because I didn't want to disagree with my dad, I joined in. Schuylar, terrified, writhed in mid-air, struggling to brace himself for his fall. He landed on his back in the scratchy pile of natural waste. Most likely in pain, and trying to make himself invisible so as to escape another round, he slinked out of the roughage with his tail tight between his legs. I think he was too scared to cry out. He took the abuse like an animal who didn't know any better. And I, misguided, mistook it for fun.

My sister was the next abuser-in-training. Soon, it became a family affair. A way we bonded. All four of us took turns throwing Schuylar in the leaves. I had no idea I was hurting my puppy. I was just grateful my parents were happy.

Schuylar soon developed a bad back. Thankfully, once my parents learned this, the throwing stopped. But it was too late. Our dog had a pinched nerve and he was terrified of us. We had broken his sense of trust and it would never be regained. When we reached out to him, he cowered away in fear.

My father, an adult, should've known better... and I'm pretty sure he did. But he was a sociopath who got his kicks out of seeing little things suffer. I don't have many regrets in my life, but I feel deep shame and remorse over this behavior. How could I not have known Schuylar was afraid of being thrown in the leaves? How could I not have known that it was hurting him? Was it possible that my perception was so completely skewed by my father's twisted laughter? By my own fear of him?

Down the Rabbit Hole

How dare he teach us this demonic version of fun. How evil of him to try and mold us into the abusive likeness of himself. It is as if he only let us get a dog so he'd have something else to abuse. I can't believe I fell for it.

As if one mistreated pet weren't enough, my mother inadvertently acquired Jack, a black lab mix. Jack was a slightly older dog whose family was moving and could not take him. My mother didn't say no to keeping Jack, which his family interpreted as, "yes, I'll take Jack," so she explained it to my father by rationalizing that maybe Schuylar would cheer up with someone to play with. But Jack proved to be the dumbest animal on the face of the earth, and Schuylar was too lazy or depressed to follow him into trouble. The two rarely acknowledged each other, let alone became best friends. Schuylar spent all of his time inside, hiding, while Jack lived mostly outdoors, trying to escape. Hey, maybe Jack was smarter than I thought...

It was as if Jack *wanted* to get hit by a car. He'd trot out into the street as soon as he saw a car approaching. He'd walk in the middle of the two-lane road, then switch lanes without reason, causing traffic to stop suddenly or swerve around him.

Down the Rabbit Hole

I would soon move to Gumma's and a few years later Schuylar would be adopted by a family friend. He was neglected at my parent's house. My mother would pass out sometimes, leaving Schuylar outside all night in the cold. No one wanted him. He was just a burden, with the peeing and pooping everywhere. So my friend's mom, who's heart broke with the knowledge of his circumstance, agreed to take him and give him a good life. The last half of his brief existence, Schuylar was loved and cared for the way he'd always deserved to be.

Jack continued to live an oblivious, but self-sufficient, life until my father had him put to sleep when he was old and too expensive to keep alive anymore. He didn't even feign upset when he took Jack to Pieper and Olsen to kill him. He couldn't have cared less.

Since I cannot change the past, I make daily living amends by being a loving mommy to my current dog. I love my Westie, Darcy, to the ends of the earth. I would never, ever dream of abusing him. He is my whole life.

The Pope recently said that all dogs DO go to heaven, so I'm comforted knowing Schuylar and Jack are there, finally at peace.

Chapter 35 — *Serial Mom*

It was the summer after 6th grade. I had been living with Gumma so I could finish out the school year in Middletown. My parents and Sibby were on tour with *Miss Saigon* so, as it was now my vacation, I flew down to Ft. Lauderdale, Florida to visit.

As usual everything was fun and games at first. We went to Disney World and Universal Studios. We ate at the Hard Rock Cafe and drove down alligator alley. Then, the fun came to a screeching halt, and my mother's true colors came through.

Denise wanted to go to a drive-in movie theatre. We didn't have those in Connecticut, and my mom wanted to experience a movie in her car while she had the chance. The movie she wanted to see was *Serial Mom*, and no, the irony was not lost on me.

Sibby, my mom and I drove to the local drive-in and parked our rental car, ready to be entertained. Promptly, after settling into a spot, my mother pulled out her flask. *Oh no,* I thought, *I don't want to be stuck here with this...*

Down the Rabbit Hole

"Sibby, let's go up on the roof," I said to my sister.

We took our blanket and laid it out on top of the car. Laying on our stomachs we proceeded to watch the dark comedy. My mother, right below me, her window down, smoked cigarettes and took swigs from her to-go container of booze.

About halfway through the movie my mother began to scoff.

"Pshh!" she let out, obviously thinking something she did not want to share.

But I knew her, and I knew the condescension that increased with each sip, er - chug, so I knew, like a child who's bottle is finished, that her flask must be empty and she was starting to whine. The movie wasn't up to her high standards of entertainment, now that she was loaded. She sighed loudly for our benefit, then shifted impatiently in her seat, finally leaning back with her foot out the window.

"This is ridiculous," she huffed, and hocked a loogie out of her window.

I couldn't continue to ignore her behavior, so I sat up.

Down the Rabbit Hole

"We can go, if you want," I said, simply giving her what she wanted.

She started the car before we'd even got off the roof.

"Oh, *can* we?" she pleaded condescendingly. "Can we, *please*?"

I did not respond as Sibby and I got back in the car. Sibby in the front seat, me in the back. I wanted to keep as far away from this beast as I could.

"Try to do something nice for you kids and you make me sit through this garbage!"

I did not bring up the fact that this had all been her idea. *You* try reasoning with a drunk.

We peeled out of the parking lot because she could not leave without letting all the other cars know how much she disliked Kathleen Turner's latest project. We began speeding home, where there was more booze.

"You really are a selfish bitch," she said, directed at me.

Down the Rabbit Hole

I remained silent, thinking how I could not escape her abuse. No matter how hard I tried to be good, she would always find a reason to fault me.

"Stupid, selfish BITCH!" she screamed, turning halfway around in her seat to wallop me.

Oh no, I worried. *She's going to get us killed.*

"I do everything for you and you're so UNGRATEFUL!"

I squashed the impulse to voice any truth and remained silent, praying to make it home in one piece. Her anger escalated. Steering the wheel with one hand, she turned around to claw at me with her other.

"You're an ungrateful, ugly, selfish little BITCH!"

She dug her nails in deep wherever her hand landed, then pulled at my skin. I was soon covered in claw marks and bleeding.

Suddenly, without warning, she swerved to the side of the road and stopped.

Down the Rabbit Hole

"Get out, get out of the car!" she pushed me into the door, trying to get me to open it.

"Mommy, no!" Sibby pleaded on my behalf.

Oh, we're doing this again, I thought. *How unoriginal.*

Without hesitation I opened the door, excited at this chance to escape forever. *Maybe **this** time I'll start a new life and never have to see this evil behemoth again.* I jumped out of the car and she sped away.

Scared, I looked around. I was on a dark residential street. There were no street lights, but there were a bunch of small, rundown houses. They were mostly dark. I was too scared to knock on any doors because, from what I could tell, this was a bad neighborhood. I started to walk. I had no idea where I was. I walked in the direction my mother's car had gone, unsure of what else to do. Two Black men passed me on the other side of the road. I saw them take notice of me, a young White girl walking alone late at night. I lowered my head and walked faster.

I took a right down a side street, hoping to find civility. The next cross street had lights and a few buildings. I approached the first building that was well-lit. It appeared to be an office building of some sort with glass windows making up the lobby. Inside, I could see a lone security guard manning the desk. I knocked on the glass. He came out from his post and unlocked the door.

"I need to use the phone. I have to call my dad. Please."

He looked confused and concerned.

"Ok, come on in. What are you doing out here all by yourself?"

"My mom abandoned me on the side of the road," I cried, looking for any way out of my life I could find.

"Oh my," he empathized. "Here - use this phone."

I went behind his desk and sat in his big office chair on wheels. I dialed my dad's theatre. The stage manager answered. After a brief hold my father's voice sing-songed.

"Y'ello."

"Dad, it's Punkie. Mom left me on the side of the road again. She's drunk. I don't know where I am."

Down the Rabbit Hole

"Oh, for Christ's sake," my father muttered, away from the phone, more to himself than to me. "Ok Punkie, I'll send a cab for you. Where are you?"

I didn't know and I didn't want him to be mad at me for not knowing, so I handed the phone to the security guard.

"Can you tell my dad where I am?" I pleaded. Caught off guard, the nice man took the phone and explained my whereabouts to my father.

Twenty minutes later a yellow cab pulled up outside. The guard let me out and I got in the taxi. I told him the address of the theatre and began to feel a little safer. I loved going to the theatre to see my dad, seeing his shows from backstage. I'd sit in his post, flying in the wings and SING! I'd sing along, at the top of my lungs, to the songs of *Miss Saigon*. I knew all the lyrics. Other stagehands would compliment me, and my dad assured me that no one in the audience could hear my belting, so it was ok for me to continue. This terrible night might turn out to be ok after all. Fun, even! I could watch the rest of the show from my dad's post and say hi to everyone in the cast. He always had sweets at his post, so I could munch on donuts or candy. Then I could go home with him and he'd be on my side, against my mother. Everything would be ok.

Down the Rabbit Hole

My dad was waiting for me at the stage door.

"Come on, I've got a cue," he hurried me.

We ran back to his post, just in time for his cue. A few minutes later, he took off his headset and walked over to me, sitting in a folding chair watching the show.

"Ok, what happened?" he asked diplomatically. I began to explain. I watched his anger rise as I described the night's events.

"Ok," he said, and went back to his switchboard.

When the show was over we made our way out of the theatre, stopping to say hello to the cast and crew. I was smiling by this time. This was the only place I ever wanted to be. I wished I could come to work with my dad every day.

We walked a few blocks to the bus stop. My smile started to fade because I knew we were headed home to my mother, the monster. My father didn't say much on our bus ride home, but I could tell his thoughts were loud.

Down the Rabbit Hole

We walked up the path to our door and I saw my mother peer out the window, anticipating either or both of us.

"Kate, why did you jump out of the car at that stoplight?" She recited a made-up alibi in an attempt to rectify the situation before my father could explode. But he was too smart to fall for her terrible acting. He grabbed her and threw her to the ground.

"YEAH!" fell from my mouth.

"You dumb CUNT!" he screamed at her.

"Eddie, no!" my victim mother cried.

"You left your daughter in the middle of nowhere AGAIN!?!"

He had clearly had enough of this.

"No, Ed, she jumped out of the car."

"She's lying!" I intercepted impatiently.

Down the Rabbit Hole

He grabbed her by her shirt and pulled her up to his face.

"You will stop this shit, you drunk, or I will divorce you!"

He dropped her. She began to cry, in a heap on the cement floor. I felt so big looking at my mother, who now felt like she had made me feel only hours earlier. I felt so confident having my dad securely on my side. I felt so much better now that he'd threatened her with divorce.

My father stormed into the bathroom, I'm sure to calm down so he didn't beat my mother to a bloody pulp. Our dwellings were a one room motel for this short-term stay, and my father had escaped to the only other room with a door, leaving me to awkwardly watch this sorry excuse for a woman, who dared to abandon me a few short hours earlier. I walked around her limp body and began to change into my pajamas. Feigning traumatic injuries, Denise picked herself off the floor and limped over to the table. She made her hands shake, as if she were so rattled from the unprompted spousal abuse that she could not light her own cigarette. She struck the spark wheel slowly so it wouldn't produce a flame, giving her reason to exhale one exasperated sigh after another, prolonging this dramatic scene. I ignored the mess, facing the other direction, looking out the window as I changed my clothes. No one said a word. Unsure of what else to do, I got into my bed, just a few feet from my parents, and

Down the Rabbit Hole

closed my eyes. The lights on, the TV on, my heart racing with adrenaline, I attempted to drown out my life and fall asleep.

Chapter 36 — Familial Alienation

I'd been hanging out with my cousin, Elizabeth Peterson, at our house on Bend lane. My parents weren't home. My dad was working, my mother was God knows where. We had spent the day gossiping, talking on the phone, and writing so-and-so loves so-and-so on the wall of my closet. Ya know, normal pre-teen stuff.

My mother came home around eight o'clock. She seemed annoyed, but what else was new? She practically ran through the back door, flung her purse on the island and threw open the refrigerator to made herself a vodka/tonic.

Elizabeth and I were in the den, right off the kitchen, right in my mother's eye-line. I could tell Denise just wanted to be alone with her drink, but she'd promised to drive Elizabeth home, so I thought I'd better intervene before she got too shit-faced to perform this task.

"Umm, Mom. Are you gonna be able to take Elizabeth home in a little while?"

Well, that did it!

Down the Rabbit Hole

"I just walked through the fucking door! Can't I have a moment's peace before you're asking me for something!?" she screamed.

She picked up her purse and stormed at me.

"You fucking ungrateful child!"

She walloped me in the head with her purse, which was oversized and full of shrapnel. I covered my face, but caught a glimpse of Elizabeth, who looked traumatized and ready to cry. *Jesus Christ,* I thought at my over-privileged cousin. *Grow up! This is nothing.*

"I'm sorry!" I apologized, cowering.

But there was no taming the beast. My mother gritted her teeth and swung her weapon even harder.

"I am so, so sick of you!" she yelled, as she began to shed tears of anger.

I held my head and shrunk to the floor. Curled up in a heap, protecting myself with my hands, I glanced at my cousin. She looked like a baby.

Down the Rabbit Hole

Watching this horrific scene seemed to have uncovered all of her innocence. Her face looked smooth, open, childlike. She was crying, but knew she was powerless over what was happening. My mother finally let up.

"Elizabeth, call your mom to come get you."

She turned quickly and went back into the kitchen to get her drink.

Elizabeth and I hurried upstairs to my room. Elizabeth was trembling.

"Oh my God, Kate!" she cried freely now that we were safely out of Denise's reach. "She just kept hitting you with her purse!" she summarized, in shock.

"I know, I know. I told you it was bad," I said a little cynically. *God, that wasn't even one of the worst beatings.*

Elizabeth picked up the phone to call her mom. I didn't want her to leave. I was scared of what was to come. It was not a good sign that this was Denise's mood at eight PM. I feared ten PM. I wished I could go to Elizabeth's for the night, but I knew Denise and Elizabeth's mom would never let me.

Down the Rabbit Hole

"I thought Denise was gonna bring you home," I heard Elizabeth's mother, Mary Jo, reply on the other end of the phone.

"She's mad," Elizabeth welled up again, "she came home and started hitting Kate with her purse!"

"Oh, for Christ's sake," I heard Mary Jo sigh. "I'll be right there."

"I want to wait outside," Elizabeth said as soon as she hung up the phone.

I felt betrayed. My cousin, my friend, wanted to get out of my house as soon as possible. She didn't want to stay with me. But *I* needed comforting! *I* was the one who just got beat up! *Your job is to console me, not run away, you selfish bitch!* But, being the people-pleaser I was, "ok," was all I said.

We tip-toed down the stairs. My mother sat at her post, the dining room table, with the TV on, probably drinking her second or third vodka/tonic.

"We're gonna wait for Mary Jo outside," I said at just the right volume and timber to keep the peace. Denise did not reply.

Down the Rabbit Hole

Elizabeth didn't speak as we stood outside waiting. She seemed far away in her own head. I felt a giant distance grow between us, and it made me feel even more alone. She couldn't wait to get away. She had no interest in my feelings, or in being there for me. She just wanted to save herself from any future trauma.

I looked next door and saw my grandmother's lights on. I wished I could sleep over there tonight, but again I knew my mother would never allow it. She was very controlling over the amount of time I spent at Gumma's house, and I'd slept over the night before. Plus, if I asked it'd give her another excuse to get mad and hit me again. I knew better than that by now. *Why didn't I save my overnight for tonight?* I silently scolded myself.

I came back to the present.

"Well, *that* was a fun night!" I joked, attempting to reconnect with my family member.

Elizabeth smiled half-heartedly, but remained silent. She craned her neck hoping that if she looked hard enough her mother's car would appear.

Down the Rabbit Hole

"We'll hafta do this again soon!" I continued, trying to make light of the heavy situation.

Again, nothing.

Why am I doing all the work here? I thought, defiantly. ***She*** *should be trying to make* ***me*** *laugh! I'm the one who just suffered the trauma! She just watched it! What a spoiled brat!*

Mary Jo finally pulled up. Elizabeth didn't even wait for the car to fully stop before grabbing the door handle to open it.

"Hi honey," Mary Jo said to me.

I envied Elizabeth for having a mom who was sober enough to drive after dark.

"Hi Mary Jo," I said and smiled, not revealing my true feelings, as usual.

"Bye Kate," Elizabeth finally spoke, still in her distant state.

"Bye," I answered, and they drove away.

Chapter 37 — Fake Diary

My mother became particularly angry when I entered puberty. Don't get me wrong - she was always angry. But something about me entering my pre-teen years *really* pissed her off. In hindsight I think she was angry at herself because when *she* was this age things really started to go off track. That's when *she* started doing drugs and having sex. So she assumed I would go down the same path. She looked at me and thought she saw herself.

Condescendingly, almost enviously, she snorted, "You're on the verge of getting your period!" as if it were disgusting, unnatural and my own poor choice. "Your hormones are raging." Clearly, she felt something I did not.

One night she sat, as usual, at the dining room table watching TV, drinking vodka/tonics and smoking cigarettes. She called me down as she often did when she was drunk, angry and feeling combative.

"You're having sex," she accused, "I know you are."

I was twelve. I was most certainly *not* having sex.

Down the Rabbit Hole

"I know what it's like to be your age. I was your age once."

She spoke with a knowing sneer that suggested that this was the age in which *all* girls start slutting it up.

"I'm not," I whispered, but she was not interested in my reply. I was there to be talked at, talked down to, corrected.

"I've read your diary. I know what you've been doing. Giving hand jobs, blow jobs, *fucking your father!*"

The air left my lungs. I knew Denise was jealous of my father loving anyone but her, but this was a new low… And she knew that. If she didn't outdo herself each time she called me downstairs to yell at me it might get boring.

"That's crazy," I whimpered. "I haven't had sex with Dad. I haven't had sex with *anyone!*"

"Yes, you have! I read it in your diary, you little slut!"

Well, she was lying. Or delusional. I hadn't had consensual sex, or even non-consensual sex, with anyone, let alone my father. I don't know what she was trying to pull. Get me to admit it, because she suspected it was true?

"You seduced Eddie! To lure him away from me! To pit him against me!"

She was shaking in anger. I stood there, frozen. The beating of the century was coming. But she took a deep breath, sat back, lit a cigarette and said those magic words.

"Get out of my sight."

I retreated, in tears, to my room, thanking God that time didn't result in a beating. I got into bed and tried to escape into sleep. An hour or so later I heard her climb the stairs. She threw open my bedroom door.

"Get into bed with me so your father can't beat me when he gets home," she ordered.

To be clear, he never hit her unless she deserved it. But what could I do?

I simply obeyed. I got into her bed and laid facing away from her. *Just go to sleep,* I told myself. But that was not her plan. She had unfinished business with me. She grabbed me by the hair.

Down the Rabbit Hole

"You little slut," she slurred, pulling me up to meet her face.

I pleaded, "No, please." But this was just the beginning.

"You fat, ungrateful little whore!"

She climbed on top of me and dug her nails into my shoulders and chest. I grabbed her hands and tried to pry her nails loose, but she just kept clawing at me.

I glimpsed my sister hiding behind the hallway wall, peering into my mother's room, afraid.

"Sibby call 911!" I screamed.

Sibby ran down the stairs and I felt a surge of power. She was going to call the police! I would be saved! I grabbed my mother by the hair, rolled over on top of her and slammed her head onto the wooden bed frame. Now *she* screamed.

"Kate, let me go!"

Down the Rabbit Hole

Her voice must've risen two octaves, which made me feel so powerful! *I was hurting her now!* I rolled off the bed, flew down the stairs, grabbed my sister and ran out the front door.

"Did you call the police?" I huffed, as we ran up the street alongside our four acre backyard.

"I dialed 911, but then I hung up because I was scared."

But I knew the police would come. I'd had enough experience with 911 to know that they always came if you called, even if you didn't even say hello. We waited by the stop sign until we spotted a cruiser. I flagged it down. The two police officers seemed surprised to see two young girls barefoot and in their pajamas in a dark field. But they pulled over and asked if we had called.

"Yes," I started to explain, "my mother is drunk and she was beating me!"

I expected much more sympathy than I was given by the emotionally detached driver of the cop car. He seemed a little annoyed, while the robotic passenger cop didn't react at all.

"Ok, get in the back."

Down the Rabbit Hole

He drove us the short distance back to our driveway and we all begrudgingly got out. As I followed them onto the front porch I decided these two were not understanding the gravity of this situation, so I warned them.

"I hope she's not getting her gun," I said.

"Your mother has a gun?" driver cop said.

"She says she does," I replied.

The four of us entered the house and found my mother sitting at the dining room table, calmly smoking a cigarette.

"We received a call from your children," driver cop reported. "Did you hit your daughter?"

"Yes, I did," Denise admitted.

She handed the officer a piece of brown construction paper folded in half with several pieces of white lined paper stapled inside: a shoddily-made journal. DIARY was written on the front in black sharpie. I craned to see what it was.

Down the Rabbit Hole

"Don't let her see it!" Denise exclaimed as the driver/officer flipped through half-heartedly. "She's been having sex. I found her diary."

"That's *her* handwriting!" I exclaimed! There was no way this trained professional was gonna fall for this! But he couldn't have been less interested.

"Is there somewhere you kids can go tonight? A relative's house or something?" My heart sunk. Once again, the people who *could* rescue me chose not to. The men who had the power to arrest my mother and take me out of that house for good had better things to do. They couldn't be bothered with all that paperwork this late at night.

My grandmother was in the hospital with chest pains, so we couldn't go next door.

"You could call my aunt, Mary Jo."

Mary Jo never wanted to get involved in family drama, but at that point we had no other choice.

"Can you call her?" the officer asked.

Down the Rabbit Hole

Why *I* was being asked to do this was beyond me, but I did it. The phone rang for a long time, but eventually Mary Jo picked up.

"It's Kate," I explained, "Siobhan and I need somewhere to stay tonight. The police are here. My mother is drunk and was beating me. Can we come to your house?"

Mary Jo was audibly inconvenienced. "Let me talk to the police officer."

I handed him the phone. While he proceeded to explain the situation at hand to my groggy aunt I awkwardly stood as far from my mother as possible. She sat, unaffected, condescendingly smoking a cigarette. She seemed to be thinking that she was winning here. She hadn't been arrested and these policemen were clearly pushovers, uninterested in protecting and serving. She couldn't have asked for a better twosome to respond to this 911 call.

"She's coming to get you," the officer said, "We'll stay with you until she gets here." Again, I questioned why they couldn't step it up, do their jobs and drive us the mile and a half, but we waited, awkwardly, the fifteen minutes or so until my annoyed aunt arrived. Meanwhile the officer who did the talking instructed us to gather some things for morning: a toothbrush, clothes, etc. He was better at the day to day than he was at wearing the pants, but who am I to judge? I was just a stupid kid.

By the time Mary Jo knocked on the door my mother had redirected her anger towards her.

"Don't you take my children!" she yelled. The two officers shifted with embarrassment. Justifiably so, seeing as how my mother was clearly still holding the power in the room despite these two men with guns.

"Denise, Jesus Christ!" Mary Jo clearly did not have time for this. "What the hell is wrong with you?"

"Kate's been having sex!" she started up again. "I read her diary!"

"She's lying!" I interrupted.

"Oh, for Christ's sake. Alright let's go," she instructed us.

"Not my baby! You can take Kate, but you leave my angel baby."

Siobhan, who was Denise's favorite by a mile, looked at the policemen awkwardly standing near the front door.

Down the Rabbit Hole

"We think it's best if both children stay with their aunt tonight. You can pick them up in the morning," they negotiated. My mother retreated. She could use a night alone, I'm sure she reasoned.

So Siobhan and I left with Mary Jo. By this time it was about 1 AM. Everyone in the Peterson household was fast asleep, so Mary Jo instructed us to be quiet as she set up a camp of sleeping bags, pillows and blankets for us in the living room. Siobhan settled in to sleep, but Mary Jo asked me to come outside to talk.

She smoked a cigarette and didn't look at me as she uncomfortably asked, "Are you sexually active?"

Was she kidding me? How could she even ask me this? I was a child trying to have a normal fucking childhood! Why was everyone so convinced I wanted to grow up so fast!? I wanted to slow down the process, for Christ's sake! I kept being forced to be an adult; all I longed for was a God damned childhood!

But all I said was "No!"

Mary Jo paused, then said, "really?"

Down the Rabbit Hole

"Yes!" I exclaimed.

I knew she wouldn't believe me. Why was I even trying to be good? It didn't matter. I should just do whatever the fuck my slutty friends were doing, for Christ sake, for as much as I was being accused of! But a little voice I like to call God spoke to me, as it often did during times I felt like this and said, *no, no. Don't retreat down that path. It'll all be ok.*

The next morning I awoke to the sounds of Mary Jo and her husband Daniel whispering while making coffee. They were being quiet, so as not to bother Sibby and me, which made me wish I had parents as considerate as them. My parents turned the volume on the TV to ten in the middle of the night, so as to wake us up with a reminder of who was bigger and more powerful. I strained to hear what Mary Jo and Daniel were saying, for I was sure it was about the night before, but I could not hear. A little while later Elizabeth and Mary came rushing into the living room.

"I wish we'd known you were here last night! We could've had a slumber party!" they said. I half-smiled, for I too wished my childhood consisted of such things.

Down the Rabbit Hole

A few hours later, after my parents awoke from their blackouts, they came to pick us up. My mother stayed in the car while my father came in and half-heartedly apologized to Mary Jo for the inconvenience. Numb, I tiptoed to the car where my mother sat, smoking a cigarette. Trying to make as little noise as possible, I slunk into the backseat behind her. We rode home in complete silence. No one said they were sorry, nor asked if Sibby and I were OK. When we got home I retreated to my room. We never spoke of the incident from the night before again.

Chapter 38 — My 13th Birthday Party

My mother and I had been planning my thirteenth birthday party for weeks. It was her idea: a big slumber party with nine of my best friends. We'd play chicken in the pool, order Dominos pizza and stay up all night playing truth or dare in our sleeping bags on the living room floor. I was so excited! See, Denise had a no sleepover rule because my friends and I kept her up all night. Yes. My friends and I. Not the cocaine she was on. It was the giggling that caused her insomnia. So I hadn't had a sleepover in years, but my mother was making an exception because entering my teens was, according to her, a big deal. We'd made cute invitations with stickers, and all nine of my BFFs had replied "yes." We'd bought streamers, balloons and a happy birthday banner. We'd ordered an Aladdin ice cream cake with 'Happy Birthday Bree,' my seventh grade nickname, written in pink icing.

'Now, wait just a minute! That doesn't sound like the mother you've been describing thus far! Isn't your mother a psycho bitch? The crazy alcoholic who leaves you on the side of the road when she's having a bad day?' Well, don't get ahead of yourself. No, Denise hadn't had a personality transplant. This party planning was all part of her master plan to ruin my life one day at a time.

Down the Rabbit Hole

The morning of what was to be the Greatest Day of My Life, my mother greeted the sunshine by throwing open her bedroom door and flying down the stairs on her broomstick, screaming that I was an ungrateful little bitch and my birthday party was cancelled. Let the record show that I had done absolutely nothing to trigger her that day. I had, in fact, been walking on eggshells all week just to avoid any potential feather-ruffling. So she had no reason whatsoever to be angry, but *you* try reasoning with a crazy person. This was how she operated. Pretending to hand you a gift and then pulling it away at the last moment. Then, to add injury to insult, slapping you in the face. It happened time and time again. I started crying, so angry with myself for falling for her fake niceness once again. I should've known better. She never gave unconditionally.

I ran next door to my grandmother's house. Gumma, who always made me feel better, hugged me and told me everything would be ok. She gave me a spare key and told me to come there after school, lock the doors behind me and draw the shades so my mother wouldn't know I was there. I felt better knowing I had somewhere safe to go, away from the wrath of my mother, but was still upset my awesome party wouldn't be happening. I went to school and cried to my friends, who had been equally as excited for my upcoming party. Everyone was so disappointed. What a terrible mother I had... But I had awesome friends. By the

Down the Rabbit Hole

end of the school day my party had been re-planned and rerouted to my friend Eve's condominium's clubhouse. Her mother knew about my home life, and she was a fair and reasonable woman. She was saving my party. Everything was ok.

I entered Gumma's house that afternoon as excited as ever about the evening ahead. I locked the doors behind me and drew the blinds. She must've been waiting for me to get home because, as feared, Denise began pounding on the doors, then the windows. I sat on the floor between the kitchen and living room, hiding, just in case she peered through a space in the Venetian blinds. Eventually she gave up. Maybe half an hour later Gumma came home. Right on cue Denise came back, but this time Gumma answered the door.

"I'm so sorry," Denise pleaded as I stood safely behind Gumma. "You can have your party. I'm so sorry I was angry this morning."

"I'm having my party at Eve's house," I boasted. "Her mom felt bad for me so she's renting out the clubhouse so I can have a birthday party."

I had foiled her plan! *She* was supposed to save the day she'd ruined. No one else was supposed to pick up her broken pieces. So she begged.

Down the Rabbit Hole

"Please let me have this party for you. I'm your mother. It's a milestone. Call Eve and tell her mother the party's back on at our house."

Maybe because I wanted to believe she'd had a change of heart. Because I wanted to believe she was sorry. Because I didn't feel I had a choice, I did as she asked. I called all of my friends and told them the fiesta was to go on as originally intended. Right back next door to the house of hell I went. As if nothing had ever happened. As if I hadn't run from my mother's screams that morning. As if I hadn't found solace in my grandmother's embrace. As if I hadn't cried into my friends' arms that day. Right back to it, just as I had done before and would do again. I returned to the problem.

My friends began to arrive an hour or so later and my mother put on her best cool mom impression. She did a really good job, too. She stayed in character all night. She acted happy as my pubescent girlfriends arrived with their sleeping bags in tow. She laughed and took pictures as we splashed and played in the pool. She pretended to be impressed as I opened presents of troll dolls and Joe Boxer shorts. If she was drinking, which I'm sure she had to have been, she hid it and grounded the wicked witch who usually appeared.

Then around nine PM, she *really* proved she was the best.

Down the Rabbit Hole

"Let's do something dangerous," she prodded, like she were the bad friend in our group.

We piled in the car and drove to the abandoned parking lot behind our house.

"Let's put two of you in the trunk at a time and do donuts around the lot!" she offered, as if she'd thoroughly planned this illegal activity.

"What!?"

"Awesome!"

"Yeah!" My friends and I exclaimed.

Abigale and I went first. Dangling our legs out of the open trunk, my probably drunk mother sped around the empty lot in circles, and we slid from side to side, as if on the Scrambler. The rest of the party stood on the sidelines marveling at how fucking cool my mother was. Their parents would never let them do this! How lucky I was to have a cool mom like this, and what was I talking about earlier at school when I called her a bitch?! She was so awesome! That's what all nine of my friends kept repeating. She was so cool! I was *so* lucky! Each pair of my friends got a good three-minute ride, while my mother laughed like a child who shouldn't have been behind the wheel. It was all the adrenaline rush we needed to keep us up all night.

My mother even managed to hold her tongue once we'd crawled into our sleeping bags and our giggling got too loud. She hollered down a few times, but her tone was more please-keep-it-down-if-you-don't-mind; and not shut-the-fuck-up-or-I'm-gonna-kill-you. She'd successfully kept the drama at bay for an entire evening. This perfect birthday only took some pre-party drama. After all, I couldn't get something for nothing. She had to take it all away from me first, so that she could have something to give back. How else would I learn that life isn't fair?

Chapter 39 — Embarrassed of What?

I always longed to be popular, so when I was in seventh grade I became a cheerleader. Cheerleaders were popular, according to *Can't Buy Me Love*, and I was determined to become Cindy Mancini, or at least Ronald once he bought his peer's approval.

It was after practice one afternoon. All the cheerleaders sat on the blacktop out front of Woodrow Wilson Middle School waiting for their rides. My father, sister and miniature dachshund Schuylar pulled up.

For some reason, my father put the car in park and got out, inviting Sibby and the dog with him. In front of my new group of trendy friends he proceeded to run around like an oversized lunatic calling, "Here Schuylar! Here boy!" Then zig-zagging away from the bounding weiner dog, prompting my sister to follow suit, laughing maniacally.

What the fuck was my father doing!?! He'd never played with Schuylar once his entire life! And I was already sitting in the car. There was no reason for this display, except to humiliate me. The other members of the squad watched this awkward scene with, what I am sure were, judgmental glares. I hid in the backseat and prayed for it to be over. A few long minutes later the family members I was ashamed to be related to got back in the car and we left. I said nothing. My father said nothing. But I could hear his thoughts. *We'll see how popular you are tomorrow.*

Ed pulled into Caliber, Inc., the local gun store, and went inside, leaving my sister and I in the car. With my father out of earshot I felt it safe to express my outrage at what had just taken place.

"How could you do that to me?" I yelled at Siobhan. "Running around with Schuylar like that in front of the whole squad! That was so embarrassing!"

I couldn't say this to my father, so my only choice was to tell my sister in the hopes that next time she suggest they leave the dog at home and pick me up quickly without any unnecessary display.

I headed straight to my room when we got home while my father and Sibby went into the kitchen to greet my mother, who was, in a rare act of motherly-ness, preparing dinner.

Seconds later I heard my father scream, "WHAAAT?!?!" as he turned into the Incredible Hulk and stomp-ran to the stairs.

Down the Rabbit Hole

I didn't know exactly why, but I knew it was because of me. In a rage he flew up the stairs and threw open my bedroom door.

"You're embarrassed of your family!?" he screamed, inches from my face, as he grabbed me by the shirt and threw me onto the bed.

Why no, what would ever give you that idea?

He picked me back up by the shirt and shoved me into the hallway where I hit the wall and fell to the floor. I tried to get up, but he was faster than me. Like a rag doll, he picked me up again and threw me down the stairs. A flight of stairs I part flew, part stumbled, down. *Would I break some bones?* I hoped so. I'd be hospitalized, and could tell them my father did it. Surely they'd take me away then! But no such luck. I hit my head on the front door. My hands trembling, I reached up and opened it.

Out I ran, headed next door to Gumma's. No one followed. Perhaps evil couldn't exist outside of my house.

I hurt. Inside and out. *Fucking Sibby! Why wouldn't she keep her stupid mouth shut? Wait until she became a pre-teen and Dad pulled the same embarrassing nonsense with her! And fucking Ed! What was he expecting? Me to be proud of his oafish hullabaloo with my wiener dog? It was natural for teenage girls to be embarrassed of their parents! He knew he was embarrassing me. He did it on purpose! To dare me to speak up, so he could assert his power over me once again. To remind me who was in control.*

I limp-ran to Gumma's, where the back door was open. She sat on the big chair watching the news as dinner simmered on the stove. *How can serenity exist only a hop, skip and a jump from hell?* I tried to open the screen door, but it was locked.

"Gumma!" I cried, as if my parent/monster were slowly stalking up behind me.

She unlocked the door and I fell into her arms. I shut both doors behind me and put on the chain lock as I tried to hurriedly explain the horror that had just transpired.

"My dad just threw me down the stairs! He told me to get out and never to come back! He's gonna kill me!"

"Oh, now! He won't as long as I have anything to say about it!" she said authoritatively, as she rocked me and stroked my hair.

Down the Rabbit Hole

This was a difficult situation for Gumma, because she hated hearing anything bad about her son. It was better when it was my mother doing all the damage because she could side with her son, who she thought was too good for Denise anyway.

The fact that her son was less than perfect was something Gumma never could accept. She heard the bad things, but refused to acknowledge them. Maybe that's where my father got it from? The need to assert himself time and time again. Perhaps it was his constant rebellion. To poke until the victim explodes with rage. To force recognition. Perhaps her lack of acknowledgement of any of his wrongdoings convinced him they were invisible. Perhaps he was fighting to be heard? Perhaps he would continue to do worse and worse things until his mother finally said the words, "OK! You're not perfect, but I still love you."

Or maybe he was just an asshole. I mean, he *was* adopted. Perhaps his birth parents were psycho serial killers. Either way, I moved in with Gumma that night. I made her come with me the next day to get clothes because I was too afraid to face my parents alone. My father was at work when we went over after school, so it was just my mother that Gumma had to protect me from. Well, and my sister, as it appeared her brainwashing against me was underway. I was sad as I gathered my things. Sad because my parents didn't want me. Sad because this was my family. Don't get me wrong, I was also thrilled to be getting out of this shithole. I had been wanting this escape my entire life and now it was becoming a reality. But there was something profoundly sad about the factors leading up to this moment. Even though they sucked, it hurt so much not to feel loved by my parents.

I lived with Gumma for almost one year. Rarely ever seeing my parents or Sibby. In fact, one day I was walking with Abigale when my mother and sister drove by. Sibby turned around in the back seat and stuck her tongue out at us. In a mean way, too, not joking. *Well, I see my mother has officially succeeded in turning my sister against me,* I thought.

I was very happy living with Gumma, but of course that happiness would not last.

Down the Rabbit Hole

Chapter 40 — Oak Park

In 1993 the national tour of *Miss Saigon* settled in Chicago for a year. My parents had friends in Oak Park, a rich suburb, so my dad decided we'd move there. At first I was devastated. I'd been living with my grandmother for almost a year at that point, so I'd been much happier. My mother interpreted my happiness as me being allowed to "run wild," so she demanded I move with them so she could keep a leash on me. After all, she didn't want to come back to the uncontrollable teenager she was convinced I was becoming.

My mother's job was to find us a home for the year. She chose a sublet that wouldn't be available until we'd already been in town for two months. So for two months my mom, dad, sister, me and our dog lived in a cramped hotel room. That's when the shit really hit the fan and my father got to see that my mother was the crazy one in the family.

My father was busy working eighteen hour days loading in the show. By the time he got home to this cozy abode my mother was already well in the bag. Only now, she turned her abuse on him.

Down the Rabbit Hole

"Shamu!" she called him. "You're so fucking fat! How could I marry such a disgusting, fat whale!?"

I laid in the bed I shared with Sibby, who could sleep through anything, and squeezed my eyes shut. My father sat on a desk chair, with his feet propped up on another, drinking his vodka/tonic and attempting to drown out her name calling.

"Denise, I just want some fucking peace and quiet."

"Oohh! Shamu just wants some peace and quiet! I just want a husband who's not a fat whale!"

My father put up with it as long as he could. He tried to ignore her, but she was determined to push him to his edge. She wanted a reaction, so finally he gave her one.

"You stupid cunt, shut the fuck up!" he finally bellowed, as he sprung from his chair and grabbed her by the hair. He threw her to the floor as she cried like the opposite of the bully she'd just been.

Down the Rabbit Hole

"Eddie, no! Don't beat me!" She cried out her favorite phrase. But it was exactly what she wanted. To prove herself the victim, to justify all of her name calling. God, my parents were twisted.

That must've been a sobering moment for my father, because he knew now that he'd hit her, Denise would call the police. Pressing charges was one of her favorite things to do. It was an opportunity to prove to people that she was the victim of an abusive husband. So he left. To the front desk in the lobby, he stumbled, to get a separate room for the night. But the damage had already been done. She was on the phone to the police and they arrived shortly thereafter. The hotel must've been booked up because he came back to a uniformed welcoming committee waiting to handcuff him.

The following day my mother was served with divorce papers. It's amazing how much one can accomplish when motivated by anger. My father was working, yet still managed to hire a lawyer and file for divorce. Denise was not happy. For some reason, as angry as she was, she was afraid of being alone. She was adamantly opposed to a divorce and my father knew that, so he used that to fight back. She'd hit him where it hurt, with drunken fat jokes; he'd hit her back in her soft spot, by taking away her punching bag and financial security.

Down the Rabbit Hole

Soon after this incident, we were to move into our sublet. My father and I agreed that Siobhan and I would stay with him in the house and Denise could find her own place to live. I didn't want to live with my abusive mother and my father paid the bills, so he got to call the shots. Although Denise was not happy about this, she was given no choice. Soon the three of us moved to the gaudiest, tackiest duplex in the John Hugh's suburb, while Denise found an apartment conveniently located above a bar in inner city Chicago. Things were looking up.

Over the next seven months, my father and I became closer. For one thing, he was consistently there, not touring with a show. For another, he cut down on his own drinking. A lot. He was showing up emotionally as well as physically.

He asked me if the things my mother had been saying about me were true. Was I sexually active?

"No!"

He believed me. He asked with compassion, not as if he already knew the answer. There was no pretense. He did not presume to know the truth. At that point he questioned if my mother had *ever* told the truth. He

Down the Rabbit Hole

started to see her for the abusive, lying drunk she really was. He was becoming a Dad.

We developed a routine. My sister and I went to school during the day, then I was responsible for her at night while Dad went to work. Oak Park was a safe town, so we'd ride our bikes down to Main street to hang out with our friends. We'd go see a two-dollar second-run movie at Lake Theatre or hang out in the park. It was like *My Girl* in the nineties.

On Mondays, my father's day off, he took us grocery shopping for food for the week, then we'd see a movie or do something fun. Family bonding time was now a part of our new and improved family.

My dad started roller blading and lost a ton of weight. He even had me take some pleasant looking pictures of him so he could open a dating profile.

But of course, my mother had to step in and ruin everything. She started insisting on visitation. My sister wanted to visit her; I did not, but for some legal reason I had to. Against my will I was forced to spend one court-ordered day with her a week.

Down the Rabbit Hole

My mother had quit drinking and entered AA. She'd gotten a job as a cashier during the graveyard shift at a local Walgreens. She told me she was sorry for all the wrong she'd done and that she wanted to make things right. She wanted her family back. She was quieter without alcohol, which had given her a voice.

She had a cute apartment in downtown Chicago, and she'd bought new clothes that were trendy compared to the uniform of jeans, tee shirts and slippers I was used to seeing her in. She seemed to be growing up. On the nights Siobhan and I would visit, she'd take us to a local all-night coffee shop, where I was introduced to cappuccino. Begrudgingly, I found myself enjoying the time I was forced to spend with her. She appeared to be making true, positive changes in her life. I was proud of her.

I suppose I was quick to forgive. I was thirteen years old and I had wanted a normal family my whole life. With my mother now sober and my father becoming a real presence in our lives, I thought everything just might work out.

One day my father sat me down and asked, genuinely, with real concern for my opinion, "Your mother wants us to give her another chance. Do you think we should?"

Down the Rabbit Hole

I thought for a second and answered, "Yes," because I wanted so badly to believe it was true. That she *had* changed and was committed to this change. That the bad things that had happened would never happen again. That we could be happy together. Like a normal fucking family.

My mother moved in shortly thereafter and the next few days were awkward, but hopeful. As if everyone were walking on eggshells thinking, "hey, maybe they won't break."

On day #6 of our reunited family I entered the house with my roller blades on. I had been out with my friends and I stopped in to get something quickly while they waited outside. I opened the back door, which led directly into the den, and found my mother on the recliner, my father on the couch, both drunk. "Hi Punkie," my father cooed. Their eyes were glassy, foggy and distant. My heart broke and I felt like a fool. *If I had just said no when he asked if we should give her another chance, he wouldn't have taken her back and this wouldn't've happened.* I was sure of it.

Of course they couldn't comfortably sit with each other sober. The damage they had done to each other hadn't been dealt with, so they had to find a way to ignore it.

Down the Rabbit Hole

A few days later, after ignoring the fact that she'd relapsed, I cautiously asked her why she was drinking again.

"It was your father's idea," she said, which surprised me. "He thinks we can just have a few." I think we both knew better.

Chapter 41 — Child See, Child Do

One day Sibby, our friend Jean, and I were in the small hotel room we lived in in Oak Park before we moved into our sublet. My mother had left piles of clean laundry on our bed and Siobhan agreed that she would put hers away before going out. I had put my clothes away, but was waiting for Siobhan to do her part so we could leave.

"Come on Siobhan, put your clothes away," I instructed hastily.

"No," she replied.

"Siobhan," I warned, "Mom told you you have to do it before we can go, so just do it!"

I raised my voice and widened my eyes. She was clearly acting up because Jean was there.

"No," Siobhan repeated.

That was it. Just as my father gave two warnings before exploding, so would I. I grabbed her with both hands.

"Siobhan, put your fucking clothes away before I beat the fucking shit out of you!"

Siobhan's arms tensed, her eyes began to fill with tears and she gritted her teeth.

"No."

Jean grew visibly uncomfortable.

"Come on guys, just stop it," she tried to smooth over the situation.

What the hell was the matter with Siobhan?! Why the fuck wouldn't she just do what she was supposed to do!?

"Siobhan!" I yelled loudly, as if that would scare her into her senses. "Just PUT YOUR SHIT AWAY!" I screamed.

Her tears began to fall. Jean looked down and away, as if she couldn't stand to watch this. I was so livid I was almost crying.

Down the Rabbit Hole

Siobhan looked me right in the eyes and whispered, "no," through her tears.

I couldn't stand this! Why did *I* have to do what Mom and Dad told me, but *she* didn't!? No way! That wasn't fair! She *would* fucking do it! I grabbed her arms again, threw her on the bed and got on top of her, digging my nails into her arms and screaming in her face.

"JUST FUCKING DO IT!!!"

"NO!" she screamed back at me. "You're not my mother!"

I pulled her off the bed and threw her against the wooden closet doors.

"OW!" she cried as she fell to the floor in hysterics.

Jean grabbed my arm. "Stop it!" she yelled at me. Jean was disturbed. I could tell she had never seen an outburst like this. *Well, welcome to my daily life,* I thought.

"You're not going anywhere," I told my mess of a sister. "We're leaving and you're staying here!" I turned and stormed out of the room.

Down the Rabbit Hole

I expected Jean to follow right behind me, but she stayed inside a moment longer to comfort Sibby. I felt guilty, but I seethed. *Why wouldn't she just put her fucking clothes away?* I thought. I couldn't understand it. *What was so fucking hard about that!?* Jean emerged and I voiced my thoughts.

"Who cares?" she answered. "What's the big deal?"

My head nearly exploded. *What do you mean what's the big deal!?!* I took a few deep breaths, but deep down I felt the truth: Jean was right. I had overreacted to a small situation. But that's what my parents did, so... I thought it was the right way to behave.

My father disciplined us with his fists. It worked on me; I responded to the fear of being hit by obeying - the way his tactic was supposed to work. My sister, on the other hand, became nervous and tense, then might *or might not* do what was being asked of her. *Sometimes* she'd complete a chore, but other times she wouldn't. My father would react by yelling louder and hitting harder. Occasionally that second round would do it and Siobhan would jump to. But sometimes even that didn't work and Siobhan would be left sobbing in a heap as our father stormed off.

Down the Rabbit Hole

As a child finding herself in the role of a parent, not knowing any other way, I adopted my father's tactic of discipline as my own. I thought it was the only way.

I was becoming the monster I hated. Because it was all I knew.

Down the Rabbit Hole

Chapter 42 — Rageaholic

I've spent a lot of my life in a "triggered state," not knowing what it was. A triggered state is when you revert back to your helpless childhood, feeling alone, afraid and powerless. I also refer to it as "falling down the rabbit hole." The deeper I fall, the harder it is to come out of.

When I was fifteen years old I went Christmas shopping with my dad at West Farms mall. West Farms is the nice mall. Meriden mall is the ghetto mall. Meriden mall has cheap knockoff clothing stores, whereas West Farms has name brands. Meriden mall would've been the appropriate place for my dad to throw a tantrum, not West Farms. Explosive outbursts are common fare at Meriden mall; people judge you at West Farms.

It was the holidays. The mall was packed. Everyone was doing their Christmas shopping. But my dad is the most impatient and important person in the world, so he cannot be made to wait. He has an agenda and if you get in his way he will cut you, metaphorically and emotionally.

We were shopping for Gumma. My dad picked out a few nice nightgowns, a bathrobe and some slippers for her and we were waiting in line

Down the Rabbit Hole

to pay. The line was taking a while. There was only one girl at the register and someone was returning something that was holding everyone else up. There were a few people ahead of us in line, also behind the girl returning something. I watched how they reacted to being held up. No one seemed mad or frustrated. One woman had a child and they were holding hands and talking. It wasn't a picturesque relationship to an outsider, but it was to me. They were just waiting. Not laughing and sharing a moment, but not making it all about them either. Just patiently shifting their weight from one foot to the other, once in a while saying something to one another.

After a few minutes of standing there in silence, my father let out an audible frustrated sigh.

"Come on!" he muttered, loud enough for everyone in line to hear. "You've got to be kidding me!"

I smiled an awkward half smile and laughed softly, trying to break the tension that was quickly forming inside him, and I started to go there. That safe place in my head where I willed a fast resolution. Maybe if I thought hard enough my energy would make another checker appear. Maybe a manager would hear my silent pleas for help and come over and quickly take care of everyone in front of us. Then my dad would be so grateful for her efficiency he'd forget his anger, thank her and be happy the rest of the trip. But no such luck. The line continued to not move, and I continued to try to solve his anger with forced smiles and what-can-you-do shrugs.

Finally, he'd had enough. Seemingly out of nowhere, my father burst like a fire hydrant. He threw down the armful of clothing he was holding, turning the heads of those ahead of us. Then, because that wasn't enough to quench his anger, he grabbed a bunch of clothes hanging on a rack next to us and threw them down on the ground as well.

"JESUS FUCKING CHRIST!" he shouted, to cap off the scene he was making. Then he stormed off.

Mortified, I scurried away in the opposite direction, so no one would think we had come in together.

I reverted back to a state of childhood helplessness, fantasizing that I was part of the family who was ahead of us in line. That was *my* mother holding *my* hand, patiently waiting to pay. I began to pretend that I was happy, that that humiliating incident had not just happened and that I was at West Farms by myself.

Down the Rabbit Hole

On autopilot I continued with the task at hand. I Christmas shopped; yes, even for my emotionally unstable father. I bought him some things he had asked for from Brookstone: an electronic back massager and a backgammon set. I bought my sister an outfit from American Eagle and Gumma some Beanie Babies. I was having a good time by myself up in my triggered fantasy life.

I began to think my dad may have left me at the mall. I hadn't seen him in forty-five minutes and I had been up and down both levels... *Maybe I've been abandoned,* I hoped. I'd pull a fun-filled *From the Mixed-Up Files of Mrs. Basil E. Frankweiler* overnight-er in the mall! I'd hide in the bathroom while security shut the place down, then try on clothes until I literally shopped 'til I dropped into a deep sleep on the coziest display bed in Filene's.

My mother would be so worried about me, and my father would be so ashamed and regretful that he'd arrive before the mall opened the next morning to retrieve me. He'd apologize profusely and promise never to explode like that again. He'd become softer, kinder, changed overnight. Like a sitcom father who sees the error of his angry ways and changes permanently in one pivotal moment. My fantasies were so comforting. I wish I could've lived in them.

Down the Rabbit Hole

It had been an hour since my father stormed off and I'd left Filene's. I figured it'd be safe to return to the scene of the crime. No way anyone still there would remember I had been with that crazy guy. I entered the store and saw my dad walking briskly towards me. My chest tightened.

"Where'd you go?" he asked impatiently.

"Uh… shopping," I replied.

He was angry. As if *I'd* run off from *him*. He shook his head as if to say, *'Jesus Christ! Last time I take you Christmas shopping!'* Then he turned and stomped out to the car. I obediently followed.

In my triggered head, I returned to my fantasy overnight adventure at the mall. I imagined raiding Mrs. Field's for a midnight snack, and trying on clothes I couldn't afford at Bloomingdales. The car ride home was silent, as we both remained deep in our rabbit holes. If only we could've addressed his childish temper. But neither of us was that brave. It was so much easier to fall down the rabbit hole, away from our problems.

Chapter 43 — Three Past Drinking Hour

Our freshman year of high school my best friend Holly and I were both dating juniors. If you were dating an upperclassman you automatically gained cool points, but if you got to go to the prom as an *under*classman you were envied.

Holly and I were so excited when prom time arrived! It would be our first prom and we'd get to go together. I started fantasizing about what kind of dress I'd get months in advance. I looked through magazines and doggy-eared dress styles I liked. My mother asked her friend Lorraine if she knew of any good dress stores and she suggested a bridal shop in Farmington. Farmington was a rich town, so we trusted that this shop would surely have gorgeous dresses. My mother agreed to take me and Holly to shop there one day after school.

The mood on the drive to Stylish Impressions was upbeat and eager. My mother engaged in my and Holly's conversation.

"What do you think your prom song will be?"

"Probably "I'll Make Love to You" by Boys 2 Men."

Down the Rabbit Hole

"Holly! Don't be stupid. They're not gonna let that be our prom song. Probably "Wild Night" by John Cougar Melloncamp."

The three of us giggled and gossiped, making the forty-five minute drive whizz by.

Unfortunately, Stylish Impressions turned out to be a big let down. Dresses were crammed onto racks with no order. The store was cluttered and the only woman working there was overwhelmed. We browsed the messy selection, but they only had a few prom style dresses to choose from. Most of their inventory looked like bridesmaid dresses from the previous decade. After maybe twenty minutes the three of us left, disappointed.

The sun had begun to set when I noticed my mother's mood darken. I glanced at the dashboard clock: five o' three. Three minutes past the start of drinking time. I tried to remain upbeat.

"Oh well, at least now we know where to get a dress if we want to get married in the eighties," I joked.

Holly laughed, but Denise remained silent. I glanced at her out of the corner of my eye and saw her chewing the inside of her cheek, deep in her head. I felt her resentment with me. *Not now,* I thought. *Not in front of my friend. We're on our way home. You'll be drunk soon enough.*

"Kate, are we going to Sam's bingo night?" Holly asked at exactly the wrong moment.

"Oh, uh, yeah. Mom, can you drop us off at Moody?" I asked, tentatively.

On the one hand, I thought she might be relieved to be rid of me for awhile so she could binge in peace. But on the other, more likely hand, I feared she'd use this request as a reason to express her pent-up rage. Of course, the latter happened. Out of nowhere she slammed on the breaks. Our Mitsubishi Mirage, which had been cruising at a steady speed of seventy miles per hour, came to a screeching halt in the fast lane of I-91 South.

"YOU'VE GOT TO BE FUCKING KIDDING ME!" she bellowed, as she turned to wallop me in the passenger seat.

I quickly turned to avoid her punches, as Holly, in the backseat, inhaled the longest audible breath of fear I've ever heard.

Down the Rabbit Hole

"Huuuuuuuuuuuuuuuuuu!" she exclaimed drawing in all of the air in the car.

I thought she was having a heart attack. Her face was white and her eyes bulged like a cartoon. *Oh Holly*, I thought. *Stop overreacting. This is nothing.*

My mother pressed on the gas petal again, but continued her tirade.

"I drive you all the way to fucking Farmington to shop for your fucking prom dresses and now you want me to drive you somewhere else?! I'm not your God damed chauffeur!"

"I'm sorry," I exclaimed, "I forgot to ask before. It's just that it's Holly's sister's school fundraiser and her parents will be there. They'll drop me off at home later. You don't have to come pick me up."

I was crying now. It seemed that I could hold in my tears until I actually had to speak. They came out with my words. My mother floored the gas petal. Holly was lurched back in her seat. She inhaled another audible gasp of fear.

Down the Rabbit Hole

"You fucking ungrateful kids! Want me to do everything for you!"

Her speed increased. Eighty… ninety miles per hour. We swerved around cars entering from the onramp. She swung in and out of lanes, passing every vehicle in our wake. I prayed we'd get pulled over by the cops. They'd see my and Holly's fear and arrest my mother for endangering our lives.

She continued to speed all the way to Moody Elementary where she slammed on the breaks in front of the school.

"Get out!" she ordered.

But Holly and I had anticipated her command by a beat and a half, already opening our car doors before she even came to a stop. She peeled off. Holly grabbed me in a hug.

"I'm so sorry, Kate! I had no idea she was gonna react like that!"

I sobbed openly. "I hate her so much!" I cried.

People who'd been making their way inside the school stopped to look at the scene unfolding.

Down the Rabbit Hole

"Come on," Holly took me by the hand and led me inside.

We walked down the empty hallway to a dark classroom. Once inside, Holly shut the door and sat with me while I let it all out.

"She just wanted to go home and drink!" I revealed the truth to my best friend. "She turns into a monster at night. She can't go a fucking second past drinking time."

Holly rubbed my back as I cried until there were no tears left.

"Do you want me to see if you can sleep over?" she offered.

"There's no way she'll let me," I answered.

I composed myself and we walked out of the classroom and into the cafeteria, where bingo night was in full swing. The fundraiser was full of seemingly happy families. Kids with both parents volunteering. Teachers dishing out pizza to smiling moms, dads and children. Why couldn't I have ended up in one of these families? Holly's dad skipped over to us.

"Hi girls! How was prom dress shopping?" he asked, chipper as always.

Down the Rabbit Hole

"Kate's mom tried to kill us," Holly replied.

Chapter 44 — Anorexia

One night I was examining myself in the mirror, grabbing my belly fat and trying to push it down, out of existence. I was fourteen years old, a freshman in high school, and one hundred and twenty one pounds. At five foot two, I was chubby.

Longing to look like a waify model, I resolved to do something about my obesity. I began popping Acutrim, walking to and from school, and not eating until dinner. But although this resulted in weight loss, it did not produce the body I was hoping for. I looked malnourished, with stick thin arms and legs and a bloated, distended midsection. This was not the heroin sheik look I was going for. It was more the look of a diabetic old man. I needed a new tactic. As if God heard my prayers, he presented me with a shortcut.

My friend Athena had a graduation party at her house. As it was night and thus time for me to eat, I indulged on a tuna sandwich in pita bread. When it was time to go home I refused the rides people offered and set out on foot. Three and a half miles of hills awaited me.

Down the Rabbit Hole

Halfway home I felt the urge to poop. *Don't stop now,* I thought, halfway up a steep incline, noting the Stop and Shop on my left, which surely had a working bathroom. *I can make it*, I cockily told myself, and pushed on. At the top of the slope, my neighborhood grocery now out of sight, I was hit with a shutter of poop chills which assured me that I had made the wrong decision. Clamping my butt cheeks together, I began sprinting on the flat road which stood before the final hill to home. *Please don't poop your pants, please don't poop your pants, please don't poop your pants,* I willed my growling bowels. Goose bumps rose up on my sweaty skin and I vowed never to pass an available restroom ever again. By the time I got home and upstairs to the bathroom it was like a poop explosion. 10,000 flushes at least! By the time the bowl had swallowed and reset, it was full of tuna fish diarrhea again. "Ahhhh," I let out the air I'd been holding onto, afraid to accidentally exhale the contents of my colon onto the sidewalk by accident. When I looked down at my stomach after my marathon bowel movement, it looked flatter than it ever had. I must've lost five pounds! That's when it occurred to me: The key to losing weight wasn't starving myself, it was extreme pooping. I could shit myself thin!

The next day I walked to Stop and Shop and bought 2 family sized boxes of Ex-lax.

Down the Rabbit Hole

Since pooping, not starving, was the way to lose weight, I began eating again. Summer was approaching and it'd be impossible to hide starving myself all day from Gumma, I reasoned. Plus, I was fucking hungry.

I began eating like a hunger strike survivor at a buffet because more eating meant more pooping which meant more weight loss. I couldn't believe I had never thought of this before! People finally envied me. "How do you stay so thin?" "I just have a fast metabolism," I was finally able to lie.

My new diet was the equivalent of throwing food directly in the toilet, only with the benefit of getting to enjoy it first. I spent a week at 4H camp that summer. Mealtimes at camp were a smorgasbord three times a day. French toast, eggs, bacon and sausage drowned in syrup for breakfast; spaghetti and meatballs covered in cheese with garlic bread for lunch; pizza and ice cream sundaes for dinner. I'd stuff myself silly, then spend a good forty-five minutes projectile shitting after.

When I got back to Gumma's house from camp, she handed me the phone. It was my father. He was in Detroit with a show, but apparently Gumma had used my absence to update him on my pooping addiction.

Down the Rabbit Hole

"How much do you weigh now?" he asked, trying to gauge the severity of my problem.

"Ninety-five pounds" I answered, stretching the truth five pounds to appear thinner and more extreme than I was. "I'm eating, though," I defended myself.

"Well, Gumma said you're taking laxatives. Pretty soon you're not going to be able to take a shit without taking a pill."

Well, I'll show Gumma! I thought. *I'll start starving again.*

The school year began and I was now a sophomore. I went back to walking to and from school and not eating until dinner time. To get back at Gumma extra hard I began adding "fasting days." Since I already only ate one meal a day I wanted to challenge myself and begin completely fasting one day a week. I was high on the power I felt from starving myself, so starving myself even more could only increase that high. After all, I didn't just want to be skinny. I wanted to look anorexic.

But Gumma was just waiting to catapult up my ass and once I refused dinner, she became extremely upset.

"If you don't eat, I'm going to report you to the school nurse," she threatened one night.

"I'm not hungry," I answered, not willing to break my fast. The next day I was called to the nurse's office.

"Your grandmother is worried about you," she said. "She says you're not eating and thinks you're losing too much weight. I want you to start coming here to get weighed every morning."

Little did she know these weigh-in's were right in line with my controlling behavior. The scale in our house was a broken antique. Now I'd be able to carefully monitor my actual number. I looked forward to seeing the number on the scale decrease every day.

Despite months of this extreme behavior I *still* did not have the body I wanted. My face and extremities were beautifully gaunt and listless, but my mid-section still swelled whenever I ate so that I looked more like an African orphan whom you could sponsor and feed for pennies a day than like a waify model. *I need to burn more calories*, I thought.

Christmas arrived and, as it was a cheat holiday, I'd allowed myself to eat freely. But, of course guilt set in once I was home and I knew I couldn't

Down the Rabbit Hole

rest until I burned the calories I'd just consumed. I decided to go for a run. It was lightly snowing so I borrowed my mother's pink sweatsuit, put on my headphones and took off like I was being chased. Down Bend Lane, up the steep hill Bartholomew Dr., a right on Reservoir Rd., then back home I sprinted, for two hours.

When I got back from my first ever run, I marveled at how much I'd sweat despite the snow. I looked at my mother and father - who, lethargically, drunkenly looked like they were becoming one with the furniture - and I felt better than them. *Look at these fatties,* I thought as I felt my stomach growl. What was that? I was hungry again! I must've burned through the gluttonous meal I'd had earlier because my body was telling me I was ready for more. *And I can have it*, I reasoned.

Maybe exercise is the key to achieving the body I want. The next morning I woke up at 5 AM and ran my new route again. Pretty soon I was doing it twice a day. Shin splints became chronic and I sweat even when I was sitting still. But, I could eat again, so it was worth it.

My legs became muscular and my body evened out. Lean and healthy, my confidence grew and my perspective of myself began to change.

Chapter 45 — Self Medicating

I got my license two weeks after turning sixteen. My parents, in an out-of-character act of generosity, gave me their old car: a beat up 1985 Mitsubishi Mirage with 200,000 miles on it. I couldn't have been more grateful. A car meant independence, and I grabbed the keys to my new freedom-mobile like I was being let out of maximum security prison. That's what it felt like, anyway.

I was a part-time busser at Farrell's Restaurant in Portland, and now I could drive myself to and from work instead of having to rely on rides from the servers. I felt so adult driving to work. Parking my car in the lot and strutting into the kitchen, car keys in hand. I'd toss them on the stainless steel counter, for all to hear. Then I'd reach into my purse for my apron and realize, oops, I'd left it in my car. Be right back, bitches! Gotta run out to my car. *My* car. My escape mechanism.

I took advantage of my ability to come and go as I pleased, without having to rely on someone else's schedule. I became Erica's ride to school every morning. Sure, we could take the bus as we had before, but how would that make the lower classmen jealous? I felt so cool parking in the student parking lot, walking up the hill to the entrance where freshman

Down the Rabbit Hole

and sophomores were being dropped off by the bus. I felt so much older than them. They were just kids, with their backpacks strapped over both shoulders. Whereas I, with fuzzy dice hanging from my rear view mirror, was mature.

It was around this time that I decided I had a crush on Cole, the new dishwasher at Farrell's. He was twenty-one and had long hair and tattoos. He smoked, so in an attempt to stealthily flirt, I pretended I did too. I bought a pack of cigarettes on my way to work and when I saw him go out on the back stoop for a smoke break, I grabbed my purse and headed out too.

"You smoke?" he asked me, surprised.

"Yeah," I said, with an air of *duh*.

We spent the next five minutes bonding as only two souls desperate enough to sit out in the cold in order to inhale toxins can. By the time he sexily flicked his butt off into the parking lot, I had agreed to smoke weed with him after work.

My shift was over at ten PM, so I hung around Farrell's for another hour. I smoked cigs on the back stoop, to keep up the facade that I was, indeed, a smoker. I drank diet cokes from the bar and answered multiple inquiries as to why I was still there.

"Oh, I told Cole I'd give him a ride home," I answered nonchalantly.

At eleven PM Farrell's closed and by eleven thirty Cole and I were in my car in the otherwise empty parking lot. I watched Cole roll a joint. He took great care in cleaning it, then breaking it up real fine. He seemed to relish this process whereas I was impatiently thinking, *Hurry up, dude. I'm gonna have to explain to Gumma why I'm home so late.* At eleven forty-five Cole finally lit the joint, and by twelve midnight my life would change forever.

I got high. And I loved it. This drug, marijuana, fit perfectly within this new chapter of my life. After just a few hits, I felt close to the person sitting next to me. Realistically, we had known each other only a few hours, but in my head we were connected on a much deeper level. I felt like I could read his thoughts and, guess what, they were all about me! Cole was in love with me, but was just too shy to say it. I wrote a story in my mind.

He wanted me around twenty-four seven, he just didn't have the nerve to ask. So, the next day I called him and gave him what he was silently asking for.

Down the Rabbit Hole

"I can come give you a ride home from work tonight," I generously offered, even though he lived just half a mile from the restaurant and I lived in another town.

"Ok," he replied.

He needed me. I was sure of it.

We began smoking pot together every time we hung out. Each night after work, we'd go back to his apartment - a one room closet with a bathroom. We'd get high and listen to Pink Floyd. We'd talk a little, fool around a lot, and spend the rest of the time in our own heads. I loved this. The thoughts I'd have about how great I was: how smart and deep. My thoughts became my friends, no longer reiterating the insults my parents beat into me. I became my biggest fan, with a man beside me wordlessly seconding my greatness.

After a few weeks, Cole spoke.

"It'd be nice if you'd start putting some money towards the pot you've been smoking."

Down the Rabbit Hole

For a split second I was hurt. Why didn't he want to take care of me? But I quickly reasoned that he was right. I *was* smoking half of his pot and he didn't make very much money. Plus, I was an independent woman with a car. I could support myself.

"Sure," I answered and gave him fifty dollars to put towards the next ounce.

I then realized that since I was buying weed, I could take it home with me and smoke it at my leisure. Sure, part of this instinct had to do with the pang of hurt I had felt when he asked me to pay for my own drugs. But mostly it had to do with the change of perspective that I longed to experience whenever I wanted.

The next night Cole pulled out our brand new ounce.

"Let's split it up fifty-fifty," I said.

I saw a pang of honesty flash in his eyes. What that probably reflected was him thinking, *Uh… but then I can't smoke it when you're not here and still act like we're contributing to it equally.* But what I chose to believe it was at the time was him thinking, *I don't want to divide our things. I want us to share everything equally.* So, I thought right back at him:

Down the Rabbit Hole

Yeah, that's right! You want me to put money towards the weed, then half of it is mine and I want it in my possession!

"Ok," was all he said.

Apparently pot causes most people to become lethargic, but for me it had the opposite effect. I became a do-er. It made me mono-focused, and whatever I did, I did with vigor. It was my junior year of high school and my schedule consisted of a plethora of English and literature classes. Taking a cue from Cole, I'd get high and read, and let me tell you, those words leaped off the page! Vivid imagery filled my once wandering mind and I became a character in the book's world. I liked reading before, but now I *loved* it. I'd get so into my nightly reading assignments that I'd often read ahead because I couldn't wait to know what happened. In my first quarter of using pot on a near-daily basis my grades went from C's and D's to A's and A+'s! Whereas once I had struggled and failed to make the honor roll, I now made high honors with ease. What a wonderful drug this pot was!

My relationship with Cole ended after about seven months, but by then I was well situated into my new lifestyle. I began attending the Academy, a magnet arts school, where I met creatives like myself who indulged in the marijuana habitually. These were my people. I was home. I embraced being out of a relationship. I filled my time with schoolwork, now determined to go to college and follow my dreams. I got a weekend waitressing job at O'Malley's, a financial and social step-up from Farrell's, so I felt more independent and secure than ever. I was living the life.

The summer before my senior year was spent outside by my pool smoking pot and reading. I read eight novels that summer, just for fun. I could not get enough of this alone time in my head. How had I never realized how smart I was? I was clearly a brilliant, capable, independent woman and I would flee this unenlightened town and head towards my dreams. Thank you pot for making my goals tangible!

The manageability continued through my senior year. I maintained straight A's and earned a Perfect Attendance award from the Academy. I was cast in both Academy productions and went the extra, non-requisite step of doing thorough character breakdowns for both roles as Athena in *Trojan Women* and Cinderella's Stepmother in *Into the Woods*. My type A personality fully revealed itself and I realized who I was: a productive pothead.

Down the Rabbit Hole

Chapter 46 — Busted

Back then, word on the street was pot wasn't addictive. At least that's what I heard, and it suited me so I repeated it whenever the subject arose. My mother was an alcoholic. *She* was the addict in the family. I just smoked pot. I was nothing like her. She got angry and violent when she drank. I was happy and productive when I was high. We were opposites. I would never be like her. That was impossible.

One day at the Academy, Chance Cox, Brett Farmer and I decided to smoke up before movement class. Movement was an awesome, hippy-dippy class where we explored different physicalities on a large open stage. Sometimes to an ambient or nature sounds tape, sometimes to our teacher Constance's direction. It was the perfect class to get high before. I mean, we were about to roll around on the floor and feel our bodies for two hours. Duh, man.

I drove to the Academy and picked up Chance and Brett in front. We drove around for a few blocks, passing a joint back and forth, then parked in the Buckley high school parking lot and rolled into class about five minutes late.

Down the Rabbit Hole

So that I won't get sued I've changed the names of some of the people involved in this story, so let's just say a classmate of mine not really named Jordan Vandersloot ran up to us.

"Constance knows you're high, guys," he said loud enough to alert the class.

"No we're not," I immediately lied.

Just deny it. They can't prove you're high, my brain reassured me. The rest of the class arrived behind Jordan, echoing his shame-on-you sentiment and relishing in our having been "caught." I looked to Chance, who had a worried admission of guilt plastered on his face, then to Brett, who looked defiant and ready to defend his behavior, and I realized we were fucked. Just then Constance appeared.

"Alright, alright. Leave the potheads alone," she said shooing the class back to the auditorium. She arrived at me. "Getting high before class, huh?" she accused.

I didn't know what to say. I was absolutely terrified. Would I be expelled? I opened my mouth to defend myself and my voice cracked. I don't even know what I was trying to say.

Down the Rabbit Hole

"Go sit down," she instructed us.

She began the day's lesson and I remained silent and in fear. How did she find out? Who told on us? It could've been a lot of people, as news traveled like lightening around the Academy. I would find out who and, so help me God, if I got expelled I would kill them. No way someone would rob me of my dream. Not before I'd even had a chance to go after it.

Constance finished her explanation of the movement exercise and we all rose to our feet to begin. I began to relax a little. She was letting the three of us participate. That was a good sign. Here I could demonstrate how pot didn't affect me the way it might affect other people. I began to move around the space. Grace, light, floating. I closed my eyes to imagine I were a feather. I felt my body become lighter and opened my eyes to a soft focus. *See,* I said to Constance in my head. *It doesn't matter that I smoked pot before class. I can still do what everyone else is doing. Better, in fact. You wouldn't have even known I was high if someone hadn't ratted on us!* Constance made her way around the class, observing and giving general direction.

Down the Rabbit Hole

"Now begin to melt," she instructed us. "Slowly, feel the weight of your body, then sink to the earth while maintaining the fluidity of your movement until you are a puddle on the floor."

"Constance, this should be slow, right?" ass-kisser Vandersloot asked.

"Yes," she answered. "Like oozing molasses, not like a ton of bricks."

"So, we should feel our weight go back to normal, then become heavier as we melt down?" I asked.

"Yes," she answered curtly. "Next time, no pot before class."

The rest of the class laughed and I felt a strong pang of defensiveness. *It wasn't a stupid question,* I thought angrily.

Our next movement class was two days later. My anxiety had subsided, as no negative consequences had followed our being humiliated in front of the class. I was confident I wasn't going to be expelled or arrested. I entered Constance's class in good spirits with the intention of laughing the whole incident off and letting bygones be bygones. But Constance had a different agenda.

Down the Rabbit Hole

"Everyone sit in a circle," she instructed. "Pot," she began, "is a very addictive drug." My heart jumped into my throat and I was triggered back into a state of helpless defenselessness. "It is absolutely not to be used before my class, or any other class for that matter."

Oh, ok, I thought. *This is just her laying down the rules. Got it. Yes ma'am.*

Constance continued, "I take my work very seriously and I expect you, as artists, to do the same and approach this work with a clear mind."

*It **doesn't** cloud my mind and I **do** take this seriously, but ok,* I thought.

"If I ever catch any of you using drugs during school hours again I will not hesitate to have you expelled. Is that clear?"

I nodded. A beat of silence followed. I looked at Brett. He was sitting defiantly with his arm slung over a bent knee, clearly biting his tongue.

Talky Vandersloot raised his hand while simultaneously starting to speak. "I just want to say I really felt threatened on Tuesday when you guys came in. I felt like our safe space was compromised."

Down the Rabbit Hole

Jesus fucking Christ, I thought. *Shut the fuck up, you brown noser! What the hell are you trying to accomplish?*

Brett snorted a condescending chortle. "What!?" he exclaimed. "Are you fucking kidding me," he echoed my sentiments aloud. Jordan looked to Constance for help. "It didn't have anything to do with you," Brett retorted. He was right. Sounded like an al-anon issue to me.

"No," Vandersloot began to defend himself, "it involved all of us because our workspace was tainted. You were all on a different level."

Brett laughed again, this time right at the suck up. "Let me ask you something. Have you ever smoked pot in my body?"

Again, Jordan looked to Constance for backup. "Obviously no," he said.

"Ok then, how do you know how I feel when I'm on it?"

"Ok," Constance finally jumped in. "This is not a debate. I've told you the rules. They are to be followed. End of discussion."

You would think that incident would've prevented me from smoking pot before the Academy again. And it did... for a few weeks. After that I was just sneakier, smoking on the drive so I had time to air out the car while still arriving on time. This was, of course, after I'd already smoked in the morning before school. And, of course, I'd smoke again at night after dinner. Smoking accompanied, or preceded, everything I did. If I was going somewhere where there would be no pot smoking, I'd be sure to smoke up first. And if there *was* smoking there, I'd pre-party by myself a little. Pot became my best friend. Always there to make me feel better.

Chapter 47 — Divorce Gift

My parent's marriage declined rapidly after getting back together in Oak Park. By the time I was sixteen, my father decided he wanted out - again. He'd finally had it - for real this time - with my mother's abusive, drunken nightly rages.

He came over to Gumma's one Saturday and asked me if I'd help him move out of the house and into Gumma's attic, which had been converted into a bedroom. Eager to repair the relationship my father and I had built in Oak Park, I said yes. They never should've gotten back together in the first place, and I'd been regretting telling him to take her back for two years now.

Never one to waste time, my father and I got to moving immediately. My mother was at work that afternoon at one of her many temporary waitressing jobs, so we were uninterrupted in our mission. A few hours later my father was settled in his new room and my mother promptly arrived home. She banged on Gumma's door.

"Kate, is your father here?"

Down the Rabbit Hole

I answered, smiling. She was scared and, apparently, blindsided. *Welcome to the wreckage of your present, bitch,* I thought. *Here's where nightly blackouts will get you.*

"Yes," I replied, as he appeared behind me.

"Denise, get out. Go home. I'm filing for divorce."

For a brief second I felt sorry for her, as a glimpse of hurt clearly flashed in her eyes before the defenses kicked in.

"Don't be ridiculous, Eddie. I'm sorry for what I said last night. I love you. Come on, come home." Her tone was condescending. She was not capable of being vulnerable for more than a heartbeat.

My father matched her patronizing with a laugh. "Oh no no no! That's it. We're done. Come on, Punkie," he said, clearly demonstrating that he loved me more than her now. He began to shut the door.

"Did you help him move, Kate!?" Denise exclaimed, blocking the door with her hand.

Down the Rabbit Hole

My father disappeared to the other room. Probably to stop himself from exploding on her. He knew better. He'd pin *her* as the violent one in this divorce.

"Yeah, he asked me to," I defended, not sure why it mattered.

"Come on, get his stuff and move it back next door," she desperately tried to persuade, as if this were all just silly nonsense.

"What? No. He doesn't want to get back with you." And again I felt briefly sorry for her. She backed down off the porch and I shut the door.

That night she probably took advantage of her new freedom. I'll bet she got rip-roaring drunk and told my sister a bunch of newly phrased lies about her real father, Buddha. I'm sure she drunk-dialed some "friends" she hadn't spoken to in years and shit out all her problems to them. Just a guess, but I'd bet the farm on it.

My father filed divorce proceedings the next day. Like I said, he does not waste time. Nor does he like things that take time, as divorces usually do. As the months passed he grew increasingly resentful. At himself, I'm sure, but he blamed it on his attorney, Julie, as if she herself were prolonging the divorce process.

Down the Rabbit Hole

Unfortunately my father's and my relationship did not automatically pick up where it left off in Oak Park. He'd grown a thicker callous since then. He did not initiate father-daughter talks like he had before. He wasn't interested in my comings and goings. He was forever impatient. Preoccupied always with the shitty circumstances of his life.

He maintained his sardonic sense of humor, however. When I asked him what he'd like for his upcoming birthday he sarcastically replied, "a divorce." So I got right on that. I was creative and at least wanted to give him a laugh. I found a small, white box and wrote the word DIVORCE on it. Then I filled the box with joke candy hearts that said things like 'fuck you' and 'bitch.' I was very proud that I'd inherited my father's twisted sense of humor. I couldn't wait for him to open it.

My grandmother always had small birthday celebrations where we'd eat ice cream cake and open presents at the kitchen table. She'd had me buy some clothes for my dad and some other things he wanted, DVDs and such. Everything was beautifully wrapped with different wrapping paper. I'd ironically wrapped the divorce in a gift bag with hearts on it.

Down the Rabbit Hole

We took pictures and I waited for the perfect moment to give him my present. Towards the end, since it was such a thoughtful gift. I handed him the bag.

"This is from me. It's what you've always wanted," I said.

He reached into the bag and pulled out the box. His face turned beet red as he read what it said. He searched for the right response.

"It's what you asked for!" I said, trying to accentuate the joke.

Gumma grimaced and averted her eyes.

"Yes, yes it is... Thank you, Punkie," he said quietly.

"It was a joke," I defended to Gumma, who was clearly embarrassed by it.

My father stood up and hugged me. A little too softly. Slightly inappropriately. As if I understood him on an adult level. I was just trying to make him laugh. No one laughed.

Chapter 48 — Vacationing With A Liar

After my father moved in with me and Gumma, I learned what the straw was that had broken the camel's back. My mother had planned to take my father and sister on a cruise on her own dime, but during a drunken night of raging had rescinded the gift, as she liked to do. Remember my thirteenth birthday party? Yeah. It was a hobby of hers. Anyway, my father was sick of being held hostage by her mood swings, so he'd finally left her. But now my mother was more determined than ever to take *someone* in her family on vacation. She had to prove that she was able to follow through on her promises.

It was the end of my junior year of high school and I'd recently decided that I wanted to go to college. My mother, in an effort to prove she was capable of performing motherly duties, had done a bit of research and discovered Flagler College in St. Augustine, Florida. This small, private college was affordable and offered a major in theatre. She'd sent away for a bunch of brochures and offered to take me for a visit as a vacation for us.

"I don't want to go with you. You'll drink," I told her honestly.

Down the Rabbit Hole

"I promise I won't," she swore. "I won't drink the whole time we're there."

It *was* only four days... and I *should* visit the college I'm considering attending... She booked our reservations.

As our trip approached I got increasingly excited. I hadn't been on a vacation in years. In fact, I'd never been on a trip that wasn't obligatory.

I started telling my friends. "My mom and I are going to Florida this summer to check out a college." That's what most of my friends were doing that summer. I wanted so badly to have a normal family like theirs. When I told Holly, she furrowed her brow.

"Are you sure you wanna go with your mom, Kate?"

I reassured her, "She promised she wouldn't drink."

Denise and I left for Florida in good spirits and on good terms with each other. Sure, we'd had our differences, but what family doesn't fight? We were determined to have a good time on this trip and leave past arguments in the past. After all, it was only four days.

Down the Rabbit Hole

Our plane landed on schedule at Jacksonville Airport where we promptly picked up our rental car. We drove the hour to St. Augustine marveling at the wind-bent trees and the ocean climate. We arrived at our hotel where we quickly checked in and dropped off our luggage. Then we immediately got to sightseeing.

St. Augustine is a touristy town. The Fountain of Youth is there, as is the Fort Castillo de San Marcos, a national monument that used to be a military prison. There are horse-drawn carriage rides and cobblestone streets, walking ghost tours and colonial style war reenactments.

But first things first. The reason we were there: to visit my future alma mater. Flagler College's main building used to be the Ponce De Leon hotel until it was donated to the college when it opened in 1968. Now the tourist attraction serves as the girl's dormitory and dining hall to Flagler students. The gorgeous Spanish renaissance architecture was clearly very well preserved and maintained. It was love at first sight for both me and my mother. I wanted to go to there.

With that settled, we took off to sightsee. We parked our car and walked up and down St. George Street. We bought souvenirs, ate ice cream and window shopped for antiques. The sun began to set and we made our way back to the hotel to shower and change before going out to dinner.

Down the Rabbit Hole

The A1A bar and grille is a lively spot we'd walked by earlier that day. It had a New Orleans-like feel with live music and outdoor seating on the balcony patio. We walked there from our hotel, continuing to smile and take in the nightlife. It was safe, not too rowdy and the air was warm. I was in love with this town.

My mother and I ate outdoors where we could both smoke. As she had promised, she didn't drink. After dinner we walked around old Spanish colonial Williamsburg. We saw the walking ghost tour and made plans to take it the following evening. Around eleven PM we returned to our hotel.

I was a daily pot smoker at this point and figured I should reward my mother with a joint since she'd been so good about not drinking. We'd smoked together a few times before. It didn't make her evil like drinking did. I didn't even equate it to drinking at all. I pulled out a joint, lit it, took a few puffs and passed it to her. She accepted, took a few tokes and passed it back. We finished the joint while planning the next day's itinerary, then turned off the lights and fell asleep.

We woke up promptly at eight the next morning, as our Flagler tour was scheduled for nine. A nice man from Administrations met us out front of the old hotel and proceeded to guide us on our very own one-on-one

Down the Rabbit Hole

campus tour. We were led inside the rotunda where he explained that the refurbished woodworking and Tiffany stained glass windows were a common tourist attraction, and I could expect to be dodging visitors' photographs during dining hall hours. "It'll get me used to evading paparazzi," I joked to my mother, who laughed.

He showed us the girls dorms, which were empty for summer. It was eerie walking through this vacant old hotel, even in daylight, and he admitted that there were rumors of the dorms being haunted. That just made me fall in love with the school even more. It was an old renaissance-style luxury hotel, where each room was different: some had wooden built-in shelves, and the top floor rooms were shorter, as if they were just an afterthought. We moved on to the auditorium, which was massive and beautiful. He explained how play productions worked and I was hooked. This cozy little school was the place for me. I could not wait to start there. Our tour lasted about an hour and a half. After which, it was time for the beach.

My mother and I had each bought new bikinis for the trip. Metaphorically backwards, hers was white and mine was black, as if *she* were the angel in the family. We stopped at a surf shop on the way and bought a boogie board, some postcards and sunscreen. Then we headed down the A1A to Crescent Beach. We drove our rental car right onto the white sands, got out and tentatively made our way into the water. This was my first time in the ocean, so I pictured Jaws swimming underneath the opaque waters, waiting for me to wade in far enough for him to eat me. But I pushed aside my silly fears and dove in. My mother awkwardly wobbled in behind me. Soon our body temperatures adjusted and we were jumping over waves and riding them back to shore. We asked a fellow beachgoer to take pictures of us as proof that we'd had a good time together. We got out and sunbathed until we were dry. After a couple of hours, we decided it was time to head back to the hotel.

As we drove northbound on the A1A my mother pointed out Cafe Iguanas on her left.

"That looks cool," she said.

"Yeah," I replied, "but they look closed. They probably don't serve lunch. It looks like more of a night spot."

A little further down the road we laughed at another divey-looking bar and grill called Nacho Mamas. The town's tackiness made me feel at home.

Down the Rabbit Hole

After we were all showered and changed, we decided to go out to an early dinner before we went on the walking Ghost Tour. My mother wanted to go somewhere nice, so we walked into Le Pavillions as they were setting up for their dinner shift. We hadn't brought anything fancy to wear, so we were severely underdressed: me in a pink tee shirt with a cat on it and cutoffs; my mother in a white tank top and elastic waistband koolats. We were seated at a table in back, so as not to get in the way of preparations for the clientele who had bothered to make reservations. I wasn't very hungry, so I just ordered a dessert and coffee while my mother ordered steak and a glass of non-alcoholic wine. It was barely five pm, the time when my mother usually began drinking. As our meal progressed, she became more and more agitated.

"I've been paying for everything on this trip," she said to me, as if trying to find a reason outside of herself for feeling annoyed. "It'd be nice if you'd pick up the check once in awhile."

You're my mother, I thought. *The parent. The adult. The caretaker. Isn't that **your** job?* But then I rationalized that she waitressed, just as I did, and neither one of us was rolling in dough. She *had* in fact paid for everything thus far, and it made me feel grown up to pay a bill, so I didn't argue. I grabbed the check when the waiter set it down and paid it in cash with my hard-earned O'Malley's money.

Down the Rabbit Hole

"Thank you," my mother said.

The sun had set and the temperature dropped, so we went back to the hotel to change into long pants and sweaters before heading out for more sightseeing. I hesitantly broke out the weed again. Hesitantly, because she still wasn't in the best mood, so I didn't know how she'd react. Would she use this as a reason to explode: *'Why can you smoke all the weed you want on this trip, but I can't drink!?'* Or as an excuse to call me out: *'You think I'm an alcoholic, look at all the weed you smoke!'* Or if she'd be grateful: *'If I can't drink at least I can smoke a little weed...'* She didn't say anything as I lit the joint. She took it and hit it when I passed it to her. We smoked in silence. It was as if she was trying to figure out how she felt and why. Her mood didn't seem to change much, but I felt better now that I was high. We left the hotel and walked the few blocks back to downtown.

I was determined to be happy. After all, I would be stuck on this trip for two more days with my mother. There was no turning back now; we had to get along. I kept smiling, thinking I could lift her spirits with my own. We approached the row of horse-drawn carriages that lined the waterfront.

Down the Rabbit Hole

"Awwww!" I cooed. "They're so pretty! How much for a ride?" I asked the man in the tux with tails and a top hat.

"Thirty dollars for forty-five minutes to an hour," he answered.

"Sold!" I broke out my wallet. This was sure to make my mother happy. Her withdrawn silence was scaring me. It meant she was deep in her head, and it was dangerous in there. Soon she'd explode in anger if I didn't coax her back to happiness.

We rode around for the next hour being schooled by our tour guide on St. Augustine's unique history. I smiled and pointed out the sights to my mother, trying to engage her. She tried to muster a smile, but was so clearly preoccupied with not drinking. The joint we had smoked hadn't curbed her appetite for alcohol; it had exacerbated it. She did *try* to smile, though. I saw her really *try* to enjoy herself.

When our ride was over, we made our way to the walking Ghost Tour. I was excited for this, and my mother had been too; at least she had been the previous evening when we'd called to book our reservations. Maybe the thrill of being scared would elicit the same high my mother got from drinking. *Maybe a shot of adrenaline will cure her poopy mood.* But alas, this was not a haunted tour where things jumped out and scare you. It

Down the Rabbit Hole

ended up being an educational walk through the cemetery and other allegedly haunted spots. It was boring, actually. We hung toward the back, behind a group of other tourists.

"I'm tired," my mother declared as the tour neared its end.

"Yeah, me too," I agreed. We made our way back to the hotel and retired for the night. Hopefully a good night's sleep was all Denise needed and she'd be better in the morning.

The following morning we had an appointment at ten AM with the Flagler College administration and financial aid people. Sleep had seemed to improve my mother's mood a bit, so we set off to complete our obligations for this trip. The Flagler staff were very nice, walking us through every step of the paperwork. At one point, we had to call my dad to get some specific figures, so my mother put on her happiest voice to let him know we were having a great trip. My mind rattled off her pathetic internal monologue: *Isn't he sorry that he didn't go on the cruise with her now? Didn't he want her back since she was obviously capable of being a good mother and implicitly, a good wife?* I don't think he bought it.

When we'd crossed the paperwork off our list of things to do, we were free to sightsee some more. We hadn't made any plans for the day, so we decided to drive across the bridge to shop at some of the surf and novelty shops we'd passed the day before. We stopped at a few t-shirt shops where you could buy four for twenty dollars. I mixed and matched until I found the perfect four, while my mother found a baby alligator skull for my father. She was really determined to get him back.

We passed Iguana's again. "Let's stop in here," my mother said, pulling into the almost vacant lot.

"They're closed," I said, hollowly.

"Someone's here, probably setting up," she replied, gesturing towards the only other car. "I just wanna check it out," she insisted.

We parked and headed inside. Turns out she was right. A single bartender greeted us as we entered. He was taking down chairs from atop the high tables.

"Hello, ladies! How are you doing on this lovely afternoon!" He continued about his work, going behind the bar to wipe down the counter.

"We're doing alright, how 'bout yourself?" My mother cordially replied, hitting it off instantly with this friendly down-to-earth drink-slinger.

Down the Rabbit Hole

"I'm doing alright too," he smiled, "just getting ready to open for business in a little bit."

"Well, we're just looking around, don't let us get in your way," she continued. "My daughter's applying to Flagler College, so we're just getting to know the town a little."

"Isn't that nice," he smiled at me. My mother took a seat on a barstool and I made my way over to the jukebox. They continued to talk, but I was now out of earshot. I looked through the music, comparing it to the jukeboxes at O'Malley's. Some modern hits, lots of classic rock. A few of the same songs. After scanning the entire rolodex, I turned back to see if Denise was ready to go. And I saw her. Drinking a vodka/tonic. A lump entered my throat, but sadness quickly gave way to rage. I walked towards her.

"Are you fucking kidding me?" I spat under my breath.

"Oh, Kate, relax. It's only one drink."

I didn't know what to do. Rage shot through my body and took over my actions. I grabbed the keys to the rental car and ran outside.

Down the Rabbit Hole

Expecting her to follow me, like a scene out of a movie, I jumped in the car and peeled out of the lot. But neither she nor the bartender appeared to try to stop me. I kept checking the rear-view mirror, but nothing. *Now what?* I thought. I didn't have a plan. I didn't know where to go. I wanted to call my dad and cry and tell him what had happened, but this was pre-cell phone, and I didn't have the hotel key so I couldn't go back to the room and call him. I drove on a bit. My mother was supposed to be worried about me when I ran out of the bar. She was supposed to instantly regret her mistake and call the police to come find me! I was supposed to drive until they pulled me over because I matched the description given by the frantic mother who had desperately called 911 to find her baby! That was how it would happen in a movie. But instead, I just drove around aimlessly until I calmed down enough to go pick her up.

About an hour later, I pulled back into the Iguana lot. I walked back inside. My mother sat there as I'd left her.

"Where'd you go?" she asked, unconcerned.

"I took the car to get away from YOU!" I couldn't believe how unaffected she was.

Down the Rabbit Hole

"Ok. You ready to go?"

"I'm driving," I stated authoritatively. She didn't argue. "You said you weren't gonna drink on this trip!" I yelled at her as soon as we were seated.

"Oh, Kate. Calm down! I had one drink," she said dismissively, although it was clear she'd had more. Shame on me for taking off, thus granting her permission to drink more. Tears welled up in my eyes. I couldn't believe what a fool I had been! How could I have believed that she'd keep her promise? She'd never kept a promise before. How could I have been so stupid? And now I was stuck with her for another twenty-four hours. She'd ruined the trip, just like I should've known she would.

We entered the hotel room. My mother went into the bathroom and I heard the shower start. I stood in a triggered state until it came to me to just leave. I didn't have to spend any more time with her than was necessary. Why should my trip be ruined by her? I could sightsee by myself the rest of the day. I took the room key and left.

I felt powerful again, like I'd initially felt taking the car. Regaining control. Reclaiming the power. She'd worry about me this time, I was sure of it. She'd come out of the shower expecting me to be there, but where'd I go? Wandering around an unknown city alone. And when I don't come home for hours and hours, I'd let her worry about me. Let the guilt start to take over and flood her mind with worry. Fuck her! Let her be lonely the rest of the trip. Let her use this time to reflect on her bad decisions.

I didn't take the car this time. I just walked. Alone in my triggered state, all up in my head, I walked and walked. I soothed myself with happy self-talk. *You're self-sufficient. In a year you'll be living here and you'll be rid of her for good. Once you're out of Connecticut, Denise's drinking can't hurt you anymore. Just one more year and you'll be an adult.* I walked along St. George street. I went into all the shops with a smile on my lonely face. I hid the facts of my present situation from the public behind a mask of faux happiness. I walked to the fort. I read the placards, but I don't remember what they said. I dove deep into self pity, like a child who is too young to comprehend facts. I kept walking. *This will be my city soon,* I talked to myself. *I'll excel at Flagler. Teachers and fellow students will marvel at my talent. I'll be the star of the school.*

Four and a half hours later I tired of walking and thinking. *I'll go back to the hotel and she'll be there in tears. She'll hang up the phone with the police, who've been searching for me, and she'll run to me, apologizing profusely for fucking up.* I was sure of it this time. I longed so much to be loved like that by my mother.

Down the Rabbit Hole

The room was dark when I entered it. She was not there. I looked outside. The rental car was gone. Triggered again, as my wish to be apologized to was shattered, I robotically began to get ready for bed. I took a shower, brushed my teeth and got under the covers with my teddy bear Radar. I turned off the lights, but could not fall asleep. I feared her arrival. She'd be mad, I was sure. If she'd been out looking for me she'd be livid that I was actually safe and sound. I'd ruined her night by disappearing. If I wasn't murdered then all I'd done was inconvenience her, and the search party she'd drummed up. She'd hit me. I tried to calm myself down, but I was wound up tight.

A few minutes later, the door opened and Denise turned on the lights. I pretended to be asleep, but I could tell by the sound of her movements that she was hammered. She stumbled to the bed next to mine, lit a cigarette and picked up the phone.

"Hello, is this the concierge?" she slurred a terrible fake Southern accent. "Oh, well, may I speak to someone with authority? Yes, I'll hold."

I began to sweat. I was livid that she'd used my disappearance as an opportunity to get wasted, and afraid she'd confront me and start a fight while she was on hold.

Down the Rabbit Hole

"Hello, are you the manager?" my mother cooed to the victim on the other end of the line. "I just wanted to complement you on your fine establishment. The gentleman behind the desk was so helpful to me today. I think it's important to recognize excellent hospitality and he was a true southern gentleman. Thank you for employing such a lovely staff."

I not only felt bad for myself now, I also felt bad for the poor on-duty night manager of this Motel 6 on the other end of the line, who had to take drunken calls from alcoholic tourists in the middle of the night. I couldn't hear his reply but I'll bet his thoughts went something like this: *Uhhh... Okaaay. Listen drunky, I've got a crossword puzzle to do so why don't you sleep it off.* I was so embarrassed to be related to her.

She hung up the phone and I tensed up again. *Please just go to sleep. Please don't start shit with me. Just go to sleep.* She went into the bathroom and I took the opportunity to adjust my "sleeping" position, as I didn't want to move in front of her, letting her know I was awake and available for verbal abuse. When she emerged from the bathroom, as if God had heard my pleas, she turned off the lights and went to sleep. When I heard her snoring I let out the tension I didn't know I was holding in my body and, eventually, fell into an agitated sleep.

Down the Rabbit Hole

The following morning I woke up in fear. Afraid to confront her about what I'd heard the night before. Afraid to have to talk to her. Afraid of her starting in with the verbal abuse. I stayed in a triggered state and robotically got ready. Our flight back home wasn't until five PM, and all I wanted to do was get away from her. She made no attempt to talk to me. We operated like strangers. We packed our bags, never speaking to each other, but desperately trying to appear fine. We went to check out and my mother, in an attempt to demonstrate how functional she was when drunk, complemented the desk staff again on their hospitality and professionalism, although she had lost her fake southern accent. Her phony politeness pushed me even deeper into my triggered state, and I held back tears.

I was terrified of the impending car ride to the airport. What would she say? Would she end up hitting me? I'd be trapped with her for an hour, unless she did like she'd done before and left me on the side of the highway. I immediately lit a cigarette. Not because I wanted one, but because it gave me something to do besides talk. Eventually she spoke.

"Ya know, Kate, you're not as smart as you think you are." Blood rushed to my face in anger and my eyes filled with tears. "You have no idea what it's like to be an adult." Oh, but I did. I had been forced into adulthood, into a motherly role towards my sister, into a self-sufficient way of life,

Down the Rabbit Hole

when I was just a toddler. I remained silent, staring out the window. "When I was your age I thought I knew everything too," she continued condescendingly. "But let me tell you something, sweetheart, you've got a lot to learn."

Down the Rabbit Hole

Chapter 49 — Honestly

The following school year I was set to go to Flagler. This conservative Catholic college had strict rules and regulations regarding drug use. If you were caught with drugs you were immediately expelled, no exceptions. Freshman were required to live on campus and RAs were instructed to conduct random room searches. There was no way I was going to risk being expelled: it was my gateway school. I planned to transfer to Emerson the following year. I'd just stop smoking pot for the year. Shouldn't be a big deal. After all, I wasn't addicted.

Sure, I missed pot. But honestly, I was fine without it. Everything was so new and different. I loved being "on my own," yet within the safety net of school. I made a bunch of new friends and was cast in three student-directed plays my first semester. Plus my workload was extremely heavy, as I chose to take all my prerequisite classes like math and history at Flagler so that once I got to Emerson I could load up on arts classes. Honestly, it wasn't a huge void being without my once-daily companion.

That being said, I did begin drinking more at Flagler. There was an awesome two dollar movie theatre within walking distance of the campus that sold pitchers of drinks to underage students and allowed smoking inside.

Down the Rabbit Hole

I fucking lived at that place. Ok. That's an exaggeration. I *wanted* to live at that place. I actually only went there maybe two to three times a month, but they were good times.

I made a lot of friends in the theatre department at Flagler and attended a fair amount of off campus parties. There was always a ton of alcohol and I indulged, heavily. If I couldn't smoke pot then I'd get drunk as often as possible. It didn't occur to me at all that this might be a problem. After all, I was in college. *Everyone* was drinking like me... right? Back then I would've answered yes, but now I look back and say, honestly, probably not.

They say drug addiction goes like this: it's fun, then it's fun with problems, then it's just problems. If I'm being *totally honest,* I would say that my addiction became fun with problems around this time.

I did some embarrassing things during my drunken times as a Freshman. Many of them involving oral sex. I let a guy I would never touch while sober go down on me on the bathroom floor of a party while in a blackout. I made out with and *almost* went down on an equally unattractive girl while wasted. I *did* go down on a girlfriend of mine who I was not attracted to while under the influence. But I never thought of these incidents as being in any way alcoholic. Never. I thought it was what everyone, or at least the cool, carefree, wild people, did in college. Honestly.

When I returned home to Connecticut, the first thing I did was get high. Literally the first thing. I entered Gumma's house, quickly kissed her hello, then claimed to be exhausted and dirty from my journey. I lugged my bags upstairs and snuck up to the attic to retrieve the weed I'd hidden over Christmas break. Oh, how nice it was to be back. This routine of smoking in Gumma's attic was what I cherished most in life. This alone time, this break, this reward. The chance to dive into the depths of my beautiful mind. I looked forward to this escape every day. Immediately I resumed my daily smoking habit.

Down the Rabbit Hole

Chapter 50 — An Untreated Disease Resurfaces

I swore I wouldn't gain the freshman fifteen in college. And I didn't: I gained the first semester thirty-five. I blame the lack of full length mirrors and the thrice daily buffet. I also blame my dad for sending humongous "care packages" filled with Funny Bones, and the vending machine conveniently located outside my door.

I had packed my first semester with difficult, time consuming, heavy workload general education classes because I planned to transfer the following year and wanted to get those out of the way. Mealtimes were my only break. I'd sit in the cafeteria for the entire two hour meal period just to socialize and procrastinate before going back to work. Gaining the weight happened so fast, but the struggle to take it off would continue for years.

I was introduced to ephedrine my freshman year of college by a roommate who'd use it to stay up all night writing papers. It gave me energy and made my head feel tingly, so I started taking four pills about four times a week. Enough to wake me up and give me some energy, but not enough to make me feel like I assume it feels to smoke crack. It wasn't until a few years later that I'd discover it could be abused to lose weight.

Down the Rabbit Hole

Over the next two years I attempted to lose the weight, not yet realizing that I could abuse "mini thins" to speed up the process. I began fasting days again in 1999 one day a week, eating whatever I wanted on non-fasting days. I managed to drop fifteen pounds, none of which came off of my huge boobs. I went to a chiropractor for back pain and he recommended breast reduction surgery. I was all for it. I had always hated my big chest and envied girls with a small frame who could wear tank tops and not look dumpy. I had the surgery in January 2000.

Amazingly, after chopping off my boobs, another ten pounds fell off me in other places. It was like the rest of my body went, *oh, we're small-framed now? Ok, let's the rest of us get on board then.*

I had been taking ephedrine periodically ever since my freshman year, but in 2000 I became addicted. See, after losing all the weight and cutting off my boobs I began to see the body I'd always wanted revealing itself. It was within reach now. I could get it, but my brain told me I'd need some synthetic assistance.

Take six pills in the morning with a large, black coffee, my eating disorder told me. *And do **two** fasting days every week instead of one.* I obeyed. It was the fall of my senior year of college and my obsession was at its peak... again. I enrolled in a ballet class on Tuesday nights. Because I wanted to look emaciated for class, I made Tuesdays one of my fasting days. Tuesday's and Thursday's. I don't know how much I weighed, but my clothes were loose, as were my bowels. My stomach was so upset from starving that on Fridays I'd have diarrhea almost immediately after eating.

At this point, I'd begun to experience the "speedy" effect of the pills, and soon six pills weren't enough to give me the high I craved. I'd move up to eight. Then nine. My heart was always racing, which meant I was always burning the maximum amount of calories, even while sitting still. I couldn't believe it'd taken me so long to realize this trick!

At our penultimate dance class my ballet teacher looked at me and said, "You've lost a ton of weight since this class started!" What a rush that gave me! Especially since I agreed. I looked like a ballerina. Small chest, thin arms and legs. Even my hips, which are naturally wide, were now narrow. I had the body I'd always wanted - a dancer's body.

Down the Rabbit Hole

Chapter 51 — From Rage to Guilt

In the summer of 1999, after my year at Flagler, I moved home to Gumma's. I was scheduled to enroll at Emerson that fall, so I spent the summer working at O'Malley's and hanging out with my cousins and, amazingly, also my sister. Sibby and I had found a common bond: we both liked pot. It helped us tolerate each other, and we hung out more around this time in our lives than we ever had before.

My sister was living with my mother at our old house on Bixby street, but their relationship was turbulent. Sibby spent many nights crashing wherever someone would have her. As Sibby grew up, her relationship with our mother became increasingly toxic. Her own mental illness developed and Denise's alcoholism progressively worsened. This is not a cocktail for a healthy mother/daughter relationship. Soon the two of them couldn't spend twenty-four hours together without the cops being called.

On this particular day, I picked Siobhan up from a friend's house in Cromwell. She and Denise had had a fight the day before which resulted in Siobhan escaping to a couch in Woodbury circle, so I agreed to accompany her to our mother's to retrieve some things before she spent the following night at Gumma's.

Down the Rabbit Hole

I pulled into the driveway of 220 Bixby Street and followed Siobhan to the door. My mother answered and Siobhan immediately began insulting her.

"I'm just here to get my stuff. Get out of my way, you damn woman! I don't need your shit!"

Denise was taken aback. Whether she was acting that way to save face, or she had been blacked out the night before so she didn't remember their last interaction, I don't know. But she was calm and even smiled and laughed, a bit embarrassed at Siobhan's outburst.

"Sibby, calm down!" I hollered, following her into the messy old house. But she was on fire.

"No! She's a stupid bitch and she can fucking go to hell for all I care!"

Siobhan continued to hurl insults as she picked up random clothes off the floor of her room and threw them into a bag. I looked at my mother and suddenly felt sorry for her. She was the weak one now. Without her liquid courage, it seemed she had no strength to fight back. She just stood there awkwardly in the kitchen, taking it.

Down the Rabbit Hole

"Where's my god damned *Vampire Bible*?!" Siobhan screamed, stomping out of her room. "You fucking stole it, I know you did!"

She accused our mother, as she started tearing through the pigsty of a living room, throwing pillows and tossing things to the floor.

"Sibby, I don't know," Denise replied, and I believed her.

"It's probably hidden under a pile of garbage in your room," I offered, trying to calm her. She stormed into Denise's room.

"No, Kate. She stole it! I know she did!" At this point my mother got angry.

"Don't you go throwing shit around in *my* room!" she ordered her youngest child. I sprinted to Denise's room.

"Come on, Siobhan, let's go," I said sternly.

I did not want this fight to escalate. I took her by the arm and led her out of Denise's bedroom, but she continued to scream insults and accusations until the two of them were face to face in the tiny kitchen. Our mother had been turned on, and now her water was starting to boil.

Down the Rabbit Hole

"Don't you ever come back here!" she warned. "You don't live here anymore! I'm putting your stuff in boxes on the side of the road!"

Yup - once you put a quarter in these two they go from zero to sixty in two seconds. Sibby smiled. This is what she wanted. A reaction.

"Fine! I don't wanna live with your bitch ass anyway!" she yelled as I pulled her onto the porch. Just then Siobhan grabbed the doorjam and spun around to hurl one final epithet, as our mother slammed the wooden door, right on her hand.

"OOOUUUU!" Siobhan screamed, the door ricocheting off her knuckles, and opening enough to expose my mother's horrified face.

The transition from enraged, estranged psycho to wounded, regretful matriarch happened in a split second.

"Oh my God, Sibby! I'm so sorry!" Our mother profusely apologized as they both burst into tears.

Down the Rabbit Hole

"OOWWW!" Siobhan continued to sob as her stance weakened and her tough exterior dissipated just as quickly and automatically as our mother's had.

My mother scooped her into her arms, holding her up and repeating, "I'm so sorry! I'm so sorry!" over and over.

The two of them looked a picture the complete opposite of ten seconds ago. I started to cry. I took Siobhan's wounded hand gently in mine. Her fingers were bruised and swollen, the skin scraped off of her bleeding knuckles.

"It's ok," I said. "It's gonna be ok."

The two of them cried. Regret poured from their eyes and mouths.

"I'm so sorry," our mother kept repeating, and I knew she meant it on a deeper level. She was so sorry they had devolved into this.

Down the Rabbit Hole

Chapter 52 — College, Part 2

I moved to Boston to attend Emerson college in 1998. I met five other students at an off-campus housing meeting and we decided to find an apartment together. I believe you're attracted to people who are like you on a visceral level. I must've sensed these fellow students' penchant for partying, because on move in day when I suggested a joint my new best friends responded by whipping out a bong, a bowl and a case of beer. Hell yeah!

Our apartment, "the G2," quickly became an addict's haven. We decorated our living room with a sampling of empty beer bottles and potpourri-ed it with a constant haze of pot and cigarette smoke. At any hour of the day or night, you could find at least one of us consuming some mind-altering substance. You never had to smoke or drink alone in our apartment because there was always someone else partaking too.

The negative consequences of my pot use started piling up around this time. I began to isolate. Not like I had before, enjoying a solo smoke in the attic, but in a broader way. I *felt* alone. Lonely. Different. Pot had begun to make me feel self-conscious, even paranoid. My head, my once loyal companion, turned on me and told me that none of my roommates liked me. *You're fat and ugly again*, my mind told me. *They don't want you to join them in the living room. In fact, they're talking about you behind your back.* I became afraid of the people I lived with because I didn't feel worthy of their friendship. I spend most of my time alone in my room. If I had to pass through the living room to go to the kitchen or bathroom, I'd mentally and physically prepare, making sure I looked presentable enough to walk by any of my peers who might be in my path. Had to make sure I wasn't giving them anything to talk about. My isolating became so frequent that it became a joke among my housemates.

"Go back to your room!" Avery would yell jokingly if I showed my face in the common area.

Embarrassed, I'd smile, then self-consciously complete my task, eager to get back to my place of lonely solace.

Thank God I was dating Puck at this time, to bump me back up into the Cool People club. Puck was thirteen years older than me and we met doing a play in Middletown the summer before my sophomore year. He had a Monday through Friday, nine-to-five job in Connecticut, so on weekends he'd drive up to Boston to visit me and pretend he was in college again. My roommates loved Puck. He was funny and social and kept our apartment decorated with fresh flowers, which he sent me non-

Down the Rabbit Hole

stop. On weekends when Puck was there I felt comfortable hanging out in the living room with my roomies. I felt accepted by them when he was there. People obviously liked *us*. But when he left I lost that confidence and returned to hiding in my room.

Back then, I ignored this feeling of estrangement. I buried myself in schoolwork and argued that I was in my room all the time because I was working. It is only in hindsight that I can see how I hid from the truth beneath a blanket of productivity. How I convinced myself that I wasn't paranoid, but was merely busy. How I smoked to escape feelings that smoking caused me to feel in the first place. How it became a daily cycle and it was becoming less and less manageable than it used to be.

I moved into an apartment in Brookline my senior year. My roommate, Todd, was a medical student at Amherst and we cohabited nicely, as the lack of a common area *forced* us both to stay in our rooms. It felt nice to be free of the awkwardness I didn't know I had felt with my old roommates. Starting fresh with a new roomie, who didn't know my story, was like a new beginning. An opportunity to improve my primary relationship with my daily drug. If Todd liked me, and approved of my pot smoking, then the negative consequences of feeling less-than would disappear... and luckily, he did both. I maintained my all-day-every-day smoking ritual without ever hearing a judgmental peep out of Todd. See, he was a drinker and, although he kept it hidden, I knew that it rendered him defenseless if he were to bring up my vice. We were the perfect enablers, and thus the perfect roommates.

My last semester at Emerson I was accepted into their Los Angeles program. Since I had no idea where to get pot in LA I figured I'd just do like I had at Flagler and stop smoking while I was there. But by this time my dependency had deepened and it proved impossible to go without my daily medicine.

During my first two weeks in LA, I fell into a deep depression, but I didn't know why. I'd call Puck in Connecticut, bawling, and I didn't know why. I thought I was homesick, even though that didn't add up. I thought I just couldn't make friends because everyone was so stuck up. It never occurred to me that my depression might actually be pot withdrawal. Not for a minute did I consider that I'd become so dependent on this substance that I simply couldn't leave the apartment without it. I couldn't socialize. I felt estranged from all of my peers. I was miserable.

Then I met Landon and Antonio.

Down the Rabbit Hole

Antonio was a fellow Emersonian and Landon was a hot guy from Oklahoma who lived at the Oakwoods temporary housing complex with his dad. They partied like me.

We met at the communal grills on one of the Oakwoods patios and got drunk together, and from that moment on we were inseparable. The three of us spent the next four months getting as fucked up as possible every night. We drank copious amounts of alcohol, smoked tons of weed and Antonio and I even did ecstasy and cocaine together whenever we could get our hands on it. We showed up hung over to our mutual internship at *The Bold and the Beautiful,* and massaged away each other's hangovers instead of interning. We went to Vegas and drank around the clock, begging a stripper to get us cocaine (she refused). It was four months of absolute debauchery. But guess what? My depression had vanished. I went from depressed to ecstatic. I'd forget to call Puck, who had helped me during my low periods, because I was too busy partying. I became a mess. But, again, it was college. That's what you're supposed to do, right? I had worked extremely hard to get to this point. It was my last semester of college and I was going to fully experience it, damnit! Yeah, fully experience it by blacking out on a nightly basis.

The week after graduation was "senior week," but for me and Antonio it was just one more week of intensive self-degradation - sorry, I mean fun.

Down the Rabbit Hole

I hadn't planned on staying in Boston for senior week, but when Antonio told me he would be there my rebellious voice piped up and argued that I deserved another 7 days of letting loose before college ended. Sure, I had planned to go home to see Puck and Gumma, but this was my last week of college, man! Stop trying to hold me down!

One of the Emerson sponsored activities was a pub crawl... I know, right? Perfect for us! We pre-smoked, as usual, then headed to the bars. After the drinking commenced all I remember was Antonio crying his eyes out telling me that he loved me, then him making out with a fat girl from my acting class, then me in a cab home telling the driver what an alcoholic mess my friend was. In my mind, I was the together one. Antonio was the mess. He was my lower companion. My addict brain morphed reality for me yet again.

Down the Rabbit Hole

Chapter 53 — Hot Mess

Once college fun times were officially over, I moved in with Puck, continued to smoke pot daily and got a waitressing job at Crumble in Hartford. This was my first serving job in an upscale restaurant and it became common for me and most of my coworkers to enjoy decompressing while imbibing after work.

One night a group of us went to The Spicy Apple, a restaurant and bar a few miles from work. After two apple martinis I felt drunk enough, but the server next to me, whose name I don't remember, ordered a third and I didn't want to let her drink alone, so I let the invisible ghost of my addiction twist my arm and ordered another one too. I don't know how I got back to my car, but I do know that once I was in it I lit a roach, thinking it would sober me up enough to drive. I was parked across the street from my work, so I reclined the seat so no one would see me. I considered taking a nap, but I had to pee, so I chugged some water, put in some eye drops and drove home. I only vaguely remember this drive.

I don't remember getting ready for bed, but I know I must have because the next morning I woke up in the guest bedroom, hanging off the futon between the mattress and the featherbed. I was naked and my pajamas were strewn like breadcrumbs, marking a path to the hamper. The hamper, a cheap dorm room style contraption that consisted of two laundry bags hanging from a flimsy plastic frame, was pushed into the wall as if someone had tried to sit in it. Embarrassed, as I walked into the master bedroom and stepped on a damp rug, I realized that someone had been me. I inspected the evidence more closely, for my ego could not readily accept that I had peed in the hamper. I was not my father. He peed on things, not me. I touched the dirty laundry. It too felt damp... but perhaps it was just cold... I picked up my pajamas, piece by piece, making my way back into the spare room. I tried to recall taking them off, moving from my and Puck's bed to the guest room, but I could not. I desperately racked my brain for an acceptable excuse for this upsetting trail of urine soaked clothing, but could find none. The truth was I had peed in the hamper in a drunken blackout.

Puck was downstairs.

"Hi," I said as I descended the stairs. "Did I pee in the hamper last night?" I asked, as if he might remember.

"I don't know. It sure looks like you tried to sit in it, though."

Down the Rabbit Hole

"I don't remember it at all," I said, still searching for a reasonable explanation.

"I could see how you would think that was the bathroom," he excused my drunken behavior. "If you turned the room this way," he gestured with his hands, "then the bathroom would be there."

My inner conscious scolded him for forgiving my abhorrent behavior.

"What worries me is that you drove like that," he continued.

Without thinking, without my ego having time to interfere, I replied, "I know."

Chapter 54 — Up, Up and Away

In 2001 I upped my daily ephedrine intake to sixteen pills a day. Unable to wake up without them, I'd take all sixteen with a large iced coffee while sitting at my computer in the morning. It'd take me around fifteen minutes to swallow all sixteen pills, as they would sometimes make me sick to the point of throwing up. During those fifteen minutes I could feel them working I assume like you'd feel crystal meth working - instantly. My grogginess would dissipate and my metabolism would increase. Sometimes I'd add an additional pill or two for an extra boost. My heart would pound so loudly I actually thought others could hear it. I was so sped up my hands would shake... but, God I was skinny! *This is the life*, I thought.

I finally had the body I'd always wanted. And it was killing me. I ate aspirin so I wouldn't have a heart attack. I knew it was just a matter of time. This couldn't continue. I was going to die. I'd developed such a tolerance that sixteen pills didn't produce the same effect anymore. I got heart palpitations and desperately feared having a heart attack or stroke. I vowed to reduce my intake. And I did. Gradually I went from taking sixteen twenty-five milligram pills a day to just six.

Down the Rabbit Hole

In 2003 I moved to LA. My friend Antonio, who was from Boston but living in LA, flew back east for Thanksgiving and we drove across the country together. I had had such terrible anxiety in the days leading up to the move that I hadn't taken ephedrine in about a week. I had my first panic attack, which lasted three days, on the drive to LA. I had to let Antonio drive because I felt like I was jumping out of my skin and I didn't think that was a safe condition to operate a two ton machine in. I sat in the passenger seat afraid the bottom was going to fall off the car, for some reason. Maybe I was going crazy.

I opened up to Antonio about my ephedrine dependency.

"You've got to stop that!" he said, more emphatically than I had anticipated. "Ephedrine will kill you!" I knew he was right.

But it wasn't that easy. I was dependent on those pills, and I was afraid that without them I'd gain weight. I couldn't risk that. After all, I was moving to LA to be an actress. Now was not the time to get off speed.

I continued with six pills a day for another year. Although their effect had diminished, I took them simply out of fear that stopping would make me fat. I maintained my weight at one hundred and fifteen pounds by doing Tae Bo and simply being twenty five. Then I met Austin.

Down the Rabbit Hole

We started dating in November 2004 and I kept my ephedrine use a secret for months. Then Terri Schiavo died. This was national news because she had been in a vegetative state since suffering cardiac arrest in 1990 at the age of twenty six. I desperately feared that that was going to happen to me. I opened up to Austin about my history with eating disorders, and revealed that I was taking ephedrine, but wanted to stop. With his help over the next few months I weaned myself off of ephedrine.

During my relationship with Austin, my eating habits improved. He was very healthy and introduced me to things like apples and natural peanut butter. The transition happened organically and, off the pills and eating better, I felt healthier than I ever had. But I still had one vice: dessert. I didn't see a problem with this, and, to be honest, I still don't. I was a healthy weight, I wasn't starving myself, I was exercising regularly, I wasn't taking speed and, other than my nightly dessert, I ate well. But Austin apparently *did* have a problem with this, and one night it came out.

"I'm going to go get some Ben and Jerry's," I announced after dinner.

"Why?" he asked.

Down the Rabbit Hole

I didn't understand the question.

"Because I want it," I answered, somewhat defensively.

"But, aren't you satiated?"

Those words triggered me. Down the rabbit hole I began to fall. First of all, words that people don't use unless they're a linguistics professor trigger me. What thirty-four year old says satiated? Secondly... **what?** What the hell does hunger have to do with Ben and Jerry's? Who even thinks that way?

"I'm not too full for dessert," I answered.

And then we argued. For four hours. During which time I reminded him that I had a long history with eating disorders and was finally at a place where I felt a healthy relationship with food. This was not helping, I said sternly. Also, it was none of his business. But he disagreed. If we were partners, he reasoned, everything I did was his business. Eventually, if I did not give up sugar, I'd gain weight. Then he wouldn't be attracted to me anymore. I know now that he has codependency issues and I should've promptly directed him towards al-anon, but at the time I was so deep in that rabbit hole that all I knew how to do was plot my revenge. I'd get my eating disorder back. Then he'd be sorry.

I decided to give ephedrine another try. I had to order them online from Canada, as they had been outlawed in the states. I hid the package from Austin and excitedly took one pill, hoping it would give me the speedy feeling I'd had way back when I'd tried it the first time. I immediately got heart palpitations. I tried again the next day, this time taking two. No dice. I had bought a large quantity to make it worth it, so I continued to try periodically until they were gone. But they had stopped working and were now only causing chest pains. Oh well. I knew a friend who could get cocaine.

I bought an eight ball from a guy I worked with, with the intention of using a little every day in order to skip a meal. For a week and a half I did just that… and boy did I like it! *You're becoming your mother*, a voice in my head told me after I snorted a line. After a quick debate with myself I flushed the rest of the cocaine and vowed to never buy it again… but I didn't keep that promise. I'd buy it again and again, reasoning that I was using it as a diet supplement, then snort a few lines, feel like I was becoming my parents, then flush the rest. The insanity, which stemmed from wanting to be thin, continued.

Down the Rabbit Hole

Chapter 55 — Opening Night

Over the years my father developed depression. Not diagnosed depression, as he was too cheap and proud to go to a psychiatrist, but it was indeed depression nonetheless. He'd stop talking to Gumma and me but sit, obtrusively, in between us in the kitchen. He'd bring his silent puss into populated areas to garner awkward attention. When we asked him what was wrong he'd mutter, "just leave me alone." He'd trudge around the house morosely doing chores until he finally left for work, when I would exhale, realizing I'd been holding my breath all day. He was the most immature sad sack you've ever had the displeasure of living with. But I felt sorry for him, and I know Gumma did too.

"I wish he could find someone to make him happy," she'd say.

"No one can make him happy. It's an inside job," I'd reply.

He would never seek help. He'd just ride out his sad spells for weeks at a time, until they inevitably ended on their own.

One year his birthday occurred during one of his despondent episodes, but Gumma wanted to forge ahead anyhow, insisting that we get him

Down the Rabbit Hole

presents and a cake like we always did. I followed her orders and got him a few nice button downs and a couple of pairs of jean shorts from Bob's. We bought him an ice cream cake from Everything Ice Cream and both got him a nice card. We set up the gifts and cake on the kitchen table and called him down from his room in the attic. He begrudgingly took his seat at the table and sulked, as Gumma and I attempted to maintain a celebratory atmosphere.

"I don't want any presents," he mumbled under his breath.

"Well, we got you some," I responded, as if he had no choice.

"Give him a gift," Gumma instructed. I handed him a beautifully wrapped short sleeved plaid shirt, which he opened with great difficulty, as if showing gratitude was physically impossible. He sat, stone faced, holding the half opened box.

"Just return everything," he sputtered to me. His eyes filled with tears and my heart broke for him. He was obviously so alone in that unstable head of his, and there was nothing we could do to alleviate his pain.

"You don't like it?" I replied, unsure of what else to say. His face got red and his tears almost fell.

Down the Rabbit Hole

Then he raged, "I DON'T WANT ANYTHING!" and threw the box to the ground. Like a spoiled brat throwing a temper tantrum, he burst out of his chair and stormed upstairs. I looked at Gumma. She was heartbroken.

I went to her side, put my arms around her and, when he was out of earshot, said, "it has nothing to do with us. He's depressed and needs professional help." A few days later I returned all of his presents.

In 2002 my father worked automation on the Broadway production of *Little Shop of Horrors*. One of my favorite memories as a kid was attending my dad's opening night parties. We'd never go see the shows from the audience, as my parents claimed tickets were too expensive, but we'd always go to the party afterward. Well, I was twenty two years old when *Little Shop* opened, and my father sprung for opening night tickets this time for me and his girlfriend Tanisha.

Of course, because he had to ruin everything, my father fell into one of his depressive states once opening night rolled around, so I was dreading driving two hours in the car with him to New York. But, like a triggered little good girl, I put on a smile and attempted to appear happy next to the oversized bummer driving the car. We didn't speak at all during the drive.

Down the Rabbit Hole

We both stayed up in our twisted thinking, AM radio serenading the sullen atmosphere.

We met Tanisha outside the theatre. She smiled at us, clearly excited for a fun night ahead.

"I'll meet you after curtain outside the stage door," was all my father said before walking away.

"Ooooooh kay," Tanisha laughed, but she was hurt by his lack of recognition.

"Oh yeah," I replied, knowingly. "He's in one of his moods. It was a long, cold drive from Connecticut."

The two of us girls walked around Manhattan a little, talking and window shopping before heading back to the theatre for show time. Thankfully I could drink, so Tanisha got a glass of wine and I slammed two before act one. At intermission I refreshed my buzz with two more overpriced cocktails. I was at least slightly more prepared for my father's bad attitude once the show had ended.

Down the Rabbit Hole

As instructed, we met my dad outside the stage door where he was waiting impatiently. Without a word we followed him as he booked towards the inexpensive parking garage he insisted on parking in, eight city blocks away. No amount of alcohol could overcome the shadow my dad's anger cast over us, as Tanisha and I ran in our heels to keep up.

Opening night parties were lavish affairs held at the nicest places whichever city we were in had to offer. *Little Shop*'s opening night event was at Tavern on the Green in Central Park. Unlike past venues, which were large all-inclusive halls with a dance floor, Tavern on the Green had many small rooms, so the cast and crew were separated by room. Seating was assigned, as opposed to first come first serve, and each room had its own small buffet and bartender.

"You've gotta be fucking kidding me!" my father shouted at a caterer who gestured him towards his designated room. "This party is for US!" That was his motto regarding opening night parties, and he made sure he said it loudly at each: "The crew- WE put in all the long hours! WE bust our asses seven days a fucking week to get this piece of shit up in time for opening night! This is OUR fucking party!" I don't know who told him that, but he was convinced. "You mean to tell me I can't sit wherever I want at my own party?!" The caterer looked scared, so I pretended not to know this crazy person and broke away from him and Tanisha.

Down the Rabbit Hole

I was determined to have a good time, so I plastered a phony smile on my face and mingled from room to room by myself, eating and drinking alone. I was reminded of the time my father caused a scene in Filene's and I spent the next hour shopping, attempting to act normal, while falling down the rabbit hole in my mind. I was in a triggered state, and no matter how much I drank or ate or pretended, I could not pull myself out of that hole. I was back in the mind of a helpless child: defenseless, helpless, alone. But at least I could *act* like I wasn't. I wouldn't give my father the pleasure of seeing that he'd upset me. I wouldn't let him win at his own game.

I managed to lose my father, and consequently Tanisha, for an hour and a half. The tavern filled up past capacity, and I noticed people waiting behind a red rope to get in as I made another lap past the entrance. Just then I saw my father bounding towards me, Tanisha in tow.

Determined to keep up the act that he hadn't ruined my good time, I smiled hugely and drunkenly slurred, "HIIIIII!"

I don't know if he bought it. All he said was, "good, we're leaving." He seemed to have cooled down a little because he said, "wait here. I'll go get the car."

Down the Rabbit Hole

Once he was out of view I lit a cigarette and read Tanisha's mind. I surmised that she was on "my father's side" so I had to keep up the happy act for her as well. "Did you have fun?" I asked.

She laugh/sighed, "Oh yeah, it was a hoot," she said sarcastically. We made eye contact and I knew her night had been ruined too.

"You could've just left," I leveled with her. "You didn't have to stay with him all night."

"Yeah.." she half admitted, but she was crestfallen.

When we dropped Tanisha off at her apartment my father gave her a kiss goodbye, so he was at least in a somewhat better emotional place than he'd been. He got back in the car and started to drive the two hours home. I closed my eyes, enjoying my buzz, and pretended to sleep, but after a few minutes he said, "well, did you have fun?" With my eyes closed, I smiled.

"Yeah!" I said, beating him at his own game.

Down the Rabbit Hole

Chapter 56 — Moving My Baggage West

I had been living with Puck for a year, but was restless. This was not what I was seeking. I had dreams that I had to follow. Gumma was holding on and I couldn't just sit around Connecticut waiting for her to die. I had to go back to LA. As difficult as it was going to be, I had to pursue my goal of becoming an actress.

I told Puck I was moving back to LA in a year and felt like a huge weight had been lifted from my chest. It was what I had to do. I don't know if he didn't think I'd end up going or if it was just so far away that it didn't upset him, but he understood. Telling him, which had been the scariest part of the plan, turned out better than I could've hoped. I felt elated. Proud of myself for being a functional stoner who would not let drugs get in the way of her dreams. Look out, LA!

I spent the next year working three jobs to save as much money as possible to move to LA with. When the day to leave finally came, Antonio arrived with his dad. We loaded my stuff onto his truck, which he was shipping out west, and got in my 1995 Toyota Camry to begin our cross country drive. I was full of anxiety so I didn't even think to mention that I had an ounce of pot in the trunk until hours into our drive. I thought Anto-

Down the Rabbit Hole

nio was gonna slam on the breaks when I told him because he grabbed my wrist and turned and looked at me suddenly and intensely with his mouth agape, as if I'd been holding a winning lottery ticket back from him. I laughed and we pulled over to retrieve my stash.

We arrived in LA and I began drinking during the day in Antonio's apartment, right off Hollywood Boulevard. It was a basement dwelling with bars on the windows and I sat in it alone as the boys went to work, smoking pot and drinking while the sun was still out like a crackhead. Depressed and full of anxiety, I was too afraid to leave the apartment by myself.

But soon Landon, Antonio and I moved into a house together. I got a job and I began doing a play. Things were happening, but I had this anxious feeling that nothing could happen fast enough.

Maybe it was all the drugs and drinking… I began attending AA. I wanted to stop drinking and meet some sober people, but I had no intention of quitting pot. I attended my first meeting at Radford Hall in Studio City, where I sat by myself and cried. I tried to compose myself, to control my sobs, but I couldn't. I bawled, and I didn't know why. My diseased brain scrambled to explain this outward pouring of emotion: I was new in town and didn't know anyone, I missed Puck and my dog and Gumma, I was anxious about how I was going to support myself. But deep down I knew it was my addiction trying to surrender. My ego just wasn't ready yet.

I attended meetings for a few months, and stopped drinking, but I didn't want to give up pot. I didn't know you had to be completely sober in order to fully participate in AA so I called Dr. Drew on *Lovelines* for clarification.

"The book says the only requirement for membership is a desire to stop *drinking*," I told the doctor.

"She's found a loophole in the program," Adam Carrolla chimed in.

"In order to fully recover you have to be free from all mind altering substances," Dr. Drew somewhat impatiently answered before hanging up on me.

So I stopped going to meetings and began drinking again. If Dr. Drew said I couldn't quit just one thing, then I might as well not even try.

That April, Puck, in an attempt to hang on to our relationship, bought me and my friend Lily tickets to Britney Spears in Massachusetts. I flew back east with pot in my underwear and Lily, her boyfriend Kyle, me and Puck smoked it on the road trip from Connecticut to Massachusetts.

Down the Rabbit Hole

We arrived in Massachusetts early so we hit a bar to get the party started. I ordered a double something to get the right amount of happy in preparation for the show. Drinking made me want to smoke pot, so I took a few more tokes off a joint right outside the concert hall before we entered, and, of course, we got more drinks before finding our section. Puck had bought us standing room, close to the stage, so since we had nowhere to set our stuff down my drink had to remain in my hand the entire time. Which meant I drank it faster. I mean, it was already halfway to my mouth. The show was over way too soon. Partly because being drunk and stoned affects my perception of time, and partly because I apparently blacked out during at least two songs.

"I wish Britney had sang "What You See is What You Get" and "Breathe on Me," I lamented to Lily on the ride home, to which she tentatively replied,

"She did."

How embarrassing. I didn't even feel the right amount of drunk or stoned and yet I had blacked out? How was that possible? I totally missed the proper buzz. What a bummer! This was a special occasion and I didn't have the right high for it.

Down the Rabbit Hole

Puck had borrowed his parent's van for the drive to Massachusetts, so we returned there, switched back to Puck's car and said goodnight to our friends. The next morning, hungover and groggy, I noticed I was missing something.

"Hey, can you tell your mom I left my Gonzo shirt in the van?"

Puck, ever the doting (ex)boyfriend, had surprised me with a cute muppet tee shirt after the show. In my drunkenness, I assumed I had left it in his parents' car and would pick it up before returning to LA later that day.

"She can't find it," he said.

That's weird. It had to be there. Where else could it be? He was in the van when he gave it to me and the only time I got out of the van... was at the 7-11...

We were smoking pot on the drive home and I got thirsty and asked Puck to get me a diet coke. While he and Kyle were in the store I had randomly decided I wanted a Cadbury cream egg and jumped out of the van to add it to my order. The shirt had been on my lap. I had been in a brown out... The only explanation was that I had dropped it on the ground and not noticed. I started to cry.

"It's ok," Puck consoled, but he knew why I was really crying. The tears were just liquid shame at being a blackout drunk.

Chapter 57 — Pushing

I was lonely, I reasoned. I just needed love. It was time to start dating someone in LA. I met Charlie in my improv class and invited him over to our house to hang out with me, Landon and Antonio in the hot tub. *I'm going to just be myself, and if he doesn't like it that's his problem,* I thought before partaking in the communal joint. I then lit up a cigarette. I only smoked three a day, I rationalized, so it shouldn't bother him. I soon found out that he had never been drunk or stoned or smoked a cigarette in all of his twenty nine years, which I found naive. But we continued to date for four months despite our differences.

"You should try weed," I suggested. "Nothing bad will happen."

He considered it, but ultimately declined.

"What does it do for you?" he asked. "It doesn't seem to change your personality at all."

I loved that he said that. "See?" I'd tell my future friends. "My sober boyfriend even said it doesn't change me."

Down the Rabbit Hole

"It gives me a slightly different perspective," I answered. It was the truth.

A few months into our relationship I moved into an apartment of my own. It was a spontaneous decision brought on by a hard crash after shrooming with my roomies. The shrooms had caused me insomnia, so I was anxious and nervous the next morning, then disoriented the whole day. By nightfall I felt like the worst version of myself and just wanted to sleep, but couldn't. I spent the whole night going in and out of consciousness, getting more and more angry at the noise my housemates were making. The morning after, as usual, Landon and Antonio's alarms were going off loudly and they were snoring right through them. I decided I had fucking had it.

Banging on the wall I shared with Landon, I screamed, "TURN OFF YOUR FUCKING ALARM!"

"I did," he automatically replied, before actually doing so.

I stormed into Antonio's room, ripped his alarm clock out of the wall and threw it on the bed.

"JESUS FUCKING CHRIST!"

Down the Rabbit Hole

I began plotting. I called a lawyer friend to ask about breaking a lease and he told me I could do so with justifiable cause. I signed the lease on a new place, down the street, that afternoon. Charlie helped move me in and, two weeks later, broke up with me.

"Something happened at work last week that really affected me and I've been looking for a way to tell you about it," he began. "Pat Morita was staying at the hotel with his family. He was here for his daughter's college graduation. The first night everything was fine. I saw the whole family leave for dinner together. They looked happy and everyone was smiling. But when I went into work the next day the whole staff was frantically looking for him because, according to his wife and daughters, he'd gone missing. We were all in the parking lot of the hotel. The police had been called, the family was crying. It was the day of his daughter's graduation and he was nowhere to be found. Managers, bell hops and even housekeepers were trying to console the family, they were hysterical... Then he appeared. He got out of a taxi and stumbled toward the group, drunk out of his mind. Everyone looked at him, shocked for a moment. Then his wife and daughters burst into tears and turned and ran into the hotel, leaving him there. He was so trashed he couldn't even form a word. The hotel staff tried to help him, but he pushed them away. *'Leave me alone,'* he tried to say. I stood there, at first trying to help, but eventually just ob-

Down the Rabbit Hole

serving this sad mess. Then he started to cry. Pat Morita, Mr. Myagi, was sobbing like a little boy."

Charlie's eyes welled up with tears as he relived this moment.

"And it just broke me. It was so sad to see this seventy year old man, drunk and sobbing, alone. It was heartbreaking to watch his family run from him and leave him alone. And I realized, I can't be with someone who drinks."

As Charlie told this story, my condescending defensiveness crept up. All the reasons that I am different from Pat Morita sprung to the front of my tongue and I began,

"You know, what you saw were the late stages of alcoholism. I barely even drink. I maybe have a few drinks a week. My main thing is pot. Pot doesn't make you belligerent like that. I'll never get like that."

I believed it too. I never thought my addiction would break me. But Charlie's decision was final and that night he collected his things and left. That night I decided to quit drinking to prove to myself that I could do it. Pot was my drug. Not alcohol. I put a note on my refrigerator that said: *Today ~ 9/15/04 ~ I quit drinking **for me**!*

Down the Rabbit Hole

I fell into such a deep depression at that point that I began doctor hunting to find one that would prescribe me an anti-depressant. I was honest and told the first doctor that I was a daily pot smoker. She told me she would not prescribe me an anti depressant while I continued to smoke pot and that I should stop. I told her I couldn't and she advised me to go to Marijuana Anonymous. She also gave me information on a sliding scale psychiatrist. Since all I wanted were happy pills I began seeing the shrink. She was not licensed to prescribe medicine so I tried my hardest to garner a recommendation for a doctor who would. On my third visit I explained/threatened that my depression was so severe that I thought I should be hospitalized. I sat, triggered and stoic, in her office as she frantically made phone calls to various mental wards in search of one who would take me immediately and without insurance. Unwilling to simply give me what I wanted, I left that office and never returned.

Three weeks later I started dating Austin. We met doing *You're A Good Man, Charlie Brown*. He was Snoopy, I was Lucy. The first time we hung out we got high in my car after our show. I remember feeling above him, as he got very child-like after smoking. He seemed naive, soft, feminine. *Lightweight*, I thought. Seeking balance, I refused an invitation back to his place, as the thought of pretending pot affected me like the first time I smoked it annoyed me. Plus, I had to work in the morning and wanted to maintain my air of productive stoner, both for myself and the benefit of this new person. *Get your shit together, buddy. Stop thinking about your feelings and pay some bills online!*

I began the relationship by explaining that I was a pot addict. I used those words. Lest he think he was dating a normal woman, I wanted him to know that I smoked pot every day and had no intention of stopping. The justification was that I did not drink and I was extremely productive while high. For a few weeks this seemed to fly. Then he brought it up.

"I don't like that you smoke pot as much as you do," he said.

Defensiveness jumped to one hundred and I exclaimed my excuses: "I told you I was a pot addict!" "I don't drink!" "I like it!" "It's none of your business!" "It doesn't affect you!" "Don't try to change me!" "This is who I am!" "I'm more productive in a day than fifty non-smokers put together!" "There are no negative side effects except that you don't like it!" "You drink and I don't give you shit about it!" And this began our years-long… argument? Discussion? Debate? Over my using.

Austin did not give up. He responded to my defensiveness with patience, for the most part, and reasonable arguments. Because I loved him and I knew deep down that I had a problem that would continue to rear its ugly head, I listened to him. And together we got my pot use down from every day to twice a week. I didn't think I could do that. I definitely could not have on my own. But we had just moved in together and, with his support, I found I could have as many as three, sometimes four, consecutive sober days.

Before dating me Austin had been about a once a year pot smoker, but once we started dating and regulating my using, he himself became a twice-a-weeker right along side me. Well, on my twenty seventh birthday he had an adverse reaction to it. We believe it was the fact that he was also taking Wellbutrin at the time and the combination of that with the pot caused this reaction, however I was also taking Wellbutrin and smoked pot and I was ok. Nonetheless, Austin's head felt very hot and tingly, then he got severe anxiety and eventually went to the emergency room. They gave him some Xanax and told him it was a panic attack, but he went on to have MRIs and a CAT scan because he was convinced it was something more serious. He began seeing neurologists who told him that there are over one hundred thousand neurotransmitters in the brain and modern science is only familiar with around one hundred of them. Since he wasn't in pain they reassured him that it wasn't life threatening and put him on Klonopin. But he decided then that he couldn't smoke pot anymore. That was fine with me, but I believe it contributed to the decline

Down the Rabbit Hole

of our relationship. I continued my twice a week habit, but felt a distance grow between us when I'd smoke and he couldn't.

We finally decided to break up after four and a half years, and I felt the loneliness I'd forgotten I was familiar with. I tried to remedy this with more pot because, with no one to babysit me, I could smoke as much as I wanted to again. But now smoking every day made me feel guilty.

A few days after Austin moved out I went to an AA meeting. I had smoked pot the two consecutive days prior and was feeling hopeless, helpless and guilty. I looked up a meeting and found that there was one a half hour later up the street from me. I took that as a sign from God. I went, and I cried. I was empty, alone and sad. I shared, got two sponsors... and stayed sober for ten days. I was scheduled to have liposuction, you see, for which they were to give me a Xanax, which one of my new sponsors said would "take me out." So I relapsed purposefully on the grounds that I would come back after I'd healed. And I did. I stayed sober for another eleven days. Then I decided I didn't want to do it anymore. I guess I had my first bad day. I called Austin, who had taken my drugs and paraphanelia, and convinced him I could go back to being the happy, productive, twice a week smoker I once was. I drove to his house and noted the AA meeting I was passing on the way. A voice inside me said, *you could go there instead. It's one day at a time. That meeting*

Down the Rabbit Hole

could get you through today. But my disease quickly rebutted: *You're not ready yet. You'll just want to use again tomorrow.* So I continued on, retrieved my weed, and, relieved, smoked it.

Down the Rabbit Hole

Chapter 58 — The Death of My Best Friend

I was a bridesmaid in a wedding when Gumma died. She had broken her pelvis three years earlier and had lost the ability to walk. When her body failed, her mind followed. She drifted deeper into dementia, as if she could not bear to live without being able to do for herself. She had been so resilient her whole life - she told me she was stepped on by an elephant once. She'd overcome a broken hip at eighty-six years old, recovering and learning to walk again, and she'd recovered from pneumonia at ninety. But once she was confined to a chair, her body too frail to heal from a broken pelvis, she declined rapidly and finally succumbed at ninety-four years old.

I'd moved back to Connecticut after college to be with her during, what I thought were to be, the final years of her life. Every day after work I took her to the grocery store or Tommy's restaurant so she could get out of the house for a bit. I'd do her laundry for her because, after suffering a broken hip, I didn't want her going up and down the basement stairs. But two and a half years later I moved to LA. It was obvious Gumma had many more years in her and continuing to postpone following my dreams was building resentment and anxiety in me. I had to go. I was racked with guilt, but I had to go.

Down the Rabbit Hole

I got a text from Tanisha on the morning of September 24, 2006: "I'm so sorry, honey!" I knew Gumma had passed. I called my dad.

"Yeah, she passed away this morning." I started to cry. "Can you come home? The funeral is Wednesday."

Austin and I checked out of our Los Gatos hotel and drove to the bride's cousin's house where the bridal party and friends were gathered.

"My grandmother passed away." I was crying. Faith, my friend, the bride, had been my roommate in college freshman year. She'd observed my almost daily phone calls with Gumma and the letters we exchanged. She knew of my tumultuous upbringing and how important my Gumma had been to me. She hugged me and told me how sorry she was. I cried harder.

Just then Faith's cousin emerged. I had not met her before and I didn't recognize her from the wedding. Had she been there? She'd've looked like a woodsy fairy, even if she hadn't been wearing huge, pink wings. Her hair was long and unkempt, her clothes loose fitting and spiritual.

Down the Rabbit Hole

"Oh, darling!" she embraced me. "You poor thing! Your grandmother is in heaven!" She reassured me as I sobbed into her arms while Faith and her family surrounded us. It felt like God was speaking to me.

She led me inside her cottage, which looked like the house Goldilocks broke into. Everything was made of wood, as if she'd built this house entirely out of the trees that used to stand in its place.

"Choose one," she opened her hands to reveal three stones. One was a blue oval/square, one was a pink heart, one was a black circle. "To remind you of your grandmother." I chose the pink heart. She had been my heart.

"Thank you." I felt safe as she cradled and rocked me, as Gumma used to do. I'd always believed in God, but never so much as in that moment.

She led me back outside. "Put these on." She gave me her wings. "Fly, darling," she instructed. I waved my arms. "Fly! You are free!"

My cousin picked me up at the airport three days later. I hadn't been able to sleep on the red eye. I put on makeup as she drove.

Down the Rabbit Hole

"Easy on the mascara there, weepy," she said. We drove straight to Biega's funeral home for the wake. We were late. Everyone turned to look at us as we entered. I went straight to the casket and knelt. I began to sob. I knew I had an audience. What choice did they have? All of their chairs faced the coffin. I touched her hands. They were cold and stiff. And what was she wearing? A gaudy 1960's blue dress with a neck scarf. She never would've worn in her life! *She'd be so upset if she were alive to see what my father had bought specifically for her to spend eternity in*, I thought.

"She's at peace now, honey," my father broke my thoughts as he came up behind me and put his hand on my shoulder. I let him comfort me. I put my head on his chest. Sylvia, Gumma's live-in nurse for the past three years, approached my other side.

"She's with your grandfather now," she said in her thick Jamaican accent.

"Are you kidding?" my father began a joke. "He's probably the reason she lived so long! '*No, keep her down there a little while longer so I can have some peace!*'" I laughed through my tears.

Down the Rabbit Hole

I wanted to spend the night reminiscing about Gumma, so I invited my cousins Mary and Elizabeth and their friend Kelsey to the hotel I was staying at. We did some cocaine and I smoked pot while they drank.

"Remember when you hit Gumma's wheel?" I reminded Kelsey of the time she hit one of the old wagon wheels Gumma'd put on both sides of the driveway. She'd felt so bad about it she'd come back into Gumma's house crying. Gumma laughed and hugged Kelsey, who was only sixteen at the time, reassuring her that it was alright.

Kelsey, high and distant, had a blank look on her face now.

"Yeah," she said shortly, then glanced at Mary for help. Mary, paranoid, was looking out the hotel door peep hole.

"Do you think someone's coming?" she replied.

I sighed. I should've known better than to turn to them for solace.

"Kate, don't you wanna go to the bar to get a drink?" Elizabeth said what they were all thinking. I did not. They left and I laid awake, high and agitated, trying to feel my feelings until I finally fell asleep.

Down the Rabbit Hole

The following night, back home in LA, Austin listened as I laughed and cried in the flood of memories I shared about my grandmother.

"I remembered the time I came home from high school and Gumma called to me from the basement. Afraid she had fallen down the stairs, I ran and flung open the door. There Gumma sat with Schoen, my black cat, and five newborn kittens! 'I think Schoen might be pregnant,' she had said only two days earlier. I was used to having fat pets 'cause Gumma overfed 'em. Looks like she'd been right. 'Go get a warm, damp towel. Not too hot,' she instructed. Together we gently washed the babies off, then built them a cozy bed of towels and blankets in an old cradle. Gumma made them baby food by diluting wet cat food with warm water and stirring it up to make a drinkable porridge. She was so gentle, so kind."

I cried. More memories came.

"My father said she used to tie a rope to the swing in the backyard so she could "push" me on the swing for hours while she sat in a chair… I remember when she and Da got me a pony for my fifth birthday. I got on that thing once and it bucked me off, right onto my back on the ground, knocking the wind out of me! I cried and told them I didn't want the horse any more, so they got rid of it… Gumma took me to get my ears pierced when I was really little, but the first one hurt so much I wouldn't let the lady pierce the other one..."

I got out everything I remembered. Every good time, the few times I'd made her mad, and vice versa. I cried until I was out of tears. Then I cried some more.

The following year I visited Notre Dame in Paris and when I entered that cathedral something swept over me and I felt the presence of God and my grandmother. I broke down into tears. I sat in a pew and felt enveloped by them, as if they were hugging me. I lit a candle for Gumma and felt her hands on my shoulders. I'd always believed in God, but never so much as in that moment.

Gumma was my best friend, and losing her hurt more than I can describe. I know that she is always with me. She is my angel now, as she was my angel when she was alive. When I think of her I feel her presence and I hear her voice. I let her continue to teach me how to be okay. She gave me everything I needed to make it on my own. I've always believed in God, but now I also believe in angels.

Down the Rabbit Hole

Chapter 59 — The Death of My Worst Enemy

November 4, 2008. The day Obama got elected. How typical for my mother to die that day. She probably timed it purposefully, to prevent me from being able to vote Democrat. *Kate won't have time to vote if she has to hop on a last minute flight to Connecticut,* I imagine her smirking as she drew her last breath.

I was waitressing a lunch shift at The Good Earth restaurant in Studio City when I got the call.

"Kate, telephone," Anna's voice rang over the intercom in the kitchen.

I swear to God, if it's Sibby calling with her version of an emergency I'll ream her a new asshole! I prematurely yelled at her in my head. I told my sister never to call me at work. Shifty from Crazy Town announcing a show at the Rainbow Room did not qualify as an emergency - I don't care if tickets *are* selling out fast!

"Hello," I said warningly into the restaurant's land line.

"Kate, it's Nana. Your mother's dying."

Down the Rabbit Hole

In spite of myself, my heart ached with pain. She started to cry - which I had never heard her do before and never would again. Automatically, instinctually, I diminished the circumstances in order to protect her.

"Oh, Nana, I'm sure she'll be fine."

Denise had been in and out of the hospital for years with various alcohol induced maladies. She was just being dramatic. But Nana disagreed.

"No! Not this time." She let her tears fall freely. "She's going to die! You have to come home!"

I sighed. I didn't want to drop everything and go home! I'd have to get my shifts covered *and* buy a plane ticket. Who was gonna pay me back for that? Would I have to stay with my dad and his white trash live-in girlfriend in my grandmother's old house that had been converted into an ashtray? Or would I have to pay for a hotel? Would he let me use his car? I was *not* going to rent one, so if I couldn't use his forget it; I wasn't going. I thought of all of the ways my forty-nine year old mother's death was inconveniencing me, but all I said was "OK," to my heartbroken Nana.

Down the Rabbit Hole

I had seen my mother a few times over the last few years. Whenever I'd go home to Connecticut she'd find a way to insert herself in my path. The last time I saw her had been two years earlier, when Gumma had died. She came to her funeral "looking like a dumpster," as my cousin lovingly put it. Her hair had been an inch of grey, then morphed into a sad brown, as if she'd given up so much that even a bottled dye, let alone a hairbrush, were too much trouble for her at this point. She was bloated and wore sweatpants because that's all she owned that would fit her suddenly puffy body. The blood vessels in her nose and cheeks had burst and she wore no makeup. She was sad and lonely, I could tell, beneath her courteous smile. She hugged me and told me she was so sorry for my loss. She was trying, and it broke my heart. I'd had no idea how close to death she herself was at that point, despite her haggard appearance.

I hung up the phone as Cindy, my big-hearted manager, flew through the swinging kitchen doors.

"My mother's dying, I have to go home," I revealed, rolling my eyes to acknowledge the ill-timing.

"What!?" she exclaimed, as if my mother and I had been close and this was a tragedy. "Oh Katie! I'm so sorry!"

Down the Rabbit Hole

I shrugged, as if to say, "Don't be. I'm fine. *I'm* sorry for the inconvenience."

"Well, you go home and don't worry about your shifts. I'll get them covered." *She* was a great mom.

I called my dad. Through an exasperated sigh I revealed the latest pain in the ass.

"Mom's dying. I have to come home. Can I stay with you?"

"What!?" he exclaimed, angrily, as if I'd been keeping secret the knowledge that she was on her way out from him. "Woah, woah, woah, back up," he yelled at me. "What do you mean she's dying?"

I got angry. *Don't condescend at me, you prick! This isn't my fault!*

"Nana just called me. Apparently she's in the hospital and she's not gonna make it this time," I short-tempered back at him. "Can I stay with you and use your car?"

I finished my double shift. I probably could've gotten out of working dinner, but I thought I'd better make money while I could, since I didn't know how many shifts I'd be forced to miss. That was, *if* I went home. I really hadn't decided yet.

I got home and rolled a joint. At least I could use this as an excuse to get high. I called my mother's nurse at Middlesex Hospital, as Nana had instructed, and she confirmed the news.

"Denise has a few days left, at most." I sighed. It was starting to feel as if I *had* to go.

"You should be there for Sibby and Nana," Austin argued. God damn it.

The next day I went to spin class and a voice-over audition before getting on a red eye to New York. Austin's uncle picked me up at La Guardia early the next morning and drove me to Grand Central, where I took the 11:07 to New Haven. Sookie, my father's trailer-bred live-in girlfriend, picked me up at the train, in my dad's Marlboro-scented Toyota and drove me to Middletown. When I took the car from her to continue my journey I noticed the gas gage on empty. What a piece of shit she was. My father sure did know how to pick 'em.

I picked up my sister at her apartment in Portland. We smoked a joint before backtracking over the bridge back to Middletown. We arrived at

Down the Rabbit Hole

our old house on Bixby Street, where my mother had been living since the divorce, at almost the exact same moment as Nana and Papa.

"Should we go to the hospital?" I asked.

"No, it's too late," Nana replied, still smiling from our hug. "She died at 9:00 this morning."

"… Oh," I replied. I felt as if the wind had been knocked out of me. A pang of remorse hit me in the chest. *Well, that sucks,* I thought. I had a feeling I had some tears to cry, and I would've liked to have cried them with her so she would've known that I forgave her and that I love her. I may not have *liked* her very much, but over the years I'd grown to identify with her and I came to realize that she had done the best she could. I was no longer as angry at her. It would've been nice to have been able to tell her that. I regretted not getting on an earlier flight. I stifled my feelings and put on an unaffected face.

"Who'd you vote for?" I asked, gesturing to the 'I Voted' sticker on Nana's blouse.

"Obama," Nana retorted defensively, daring me to question her sudden liberal change of heart.

Down the Rabbit Hole

Siobhan unlocked the heavy, wooden door to my mother's house and swung it open to reveal a hoarder's wet dream. The cheap, white roller shades were drawn throughout, as if the inhabitant were paranoid someone was trying to peer in every window. A heaping pile of mail sat atop the dining room table, framed by cigarette ashes and dust. My mother's kitchen chair had a large hole in the cushion from overuse. Our old portable dishwasher, which hooked up to the faucet by a hose, was obtrusively parked in the center of the small kitchen. The garbage overflowed and the sink sat full of dirty dishes. Although the house had been empty for days, the stale smell of cigarette smoke permeated the air. I switched on a light. I should've left it off.

"Jesus," Papa exhaled, ashamed of his daughter. She had given up long ago. This mess took time to build.

I headed straight for my mother's room to look for drugs. God, I hoped I'd find cocaine! Siobhan was right behind me. I opened the top dresser drawer, where my parents used to hide their stash, and dug through the trough of old, period-stained panties, but no coke mirror hid below. Further snooping only revealed more worn, wrinkled clothing, but no drugs. Of course not. A true addict never leaves anything behind.

Down the Rabbit Hole

Siobhan held up a jewelry box that my father had given my mother. It looked like a miniature armoire, with hooks to hold necklaces and a drawer below for rings.

"Mom said I could have her engagement ring," Sibby revealed, as she looked for it.

In her sad denouement, my mother had reconnected with her high school sweetheart - the one who'd knocked her up twice - and they'd gotten "engaged." He'd given her a cheap, fake ring with gold plating and a green, plastic "stone." It was hideous, but Denise must've convinced Sibby that it was nice, because my sister got angry when she couldn't find it.

"She's probably still wearing it, Sibby," I reasoned with her. "We'll get it off her before she's cremated." Again, in spite of myself, I felt sad.

Nana rounded the corner. "We're going to go. This is just too much for me." I could tell if she didn't leave soon she'd start to cry again. This house was death.

"What about her car?" Papa hollered.

Down the Rabbit Hole

"Who's car?" Nana asked, as she hugged me and Sibby goodbye.

"… The one who died," Papa replied. He'd forgotten her name.

"Sibby's going to take it," Nana answered.

I mentally added that to the list of things to do in the short three days I'd allotted myself: *Take Sibby to the DMV to get the title transferred.*

My father showed up a few minutes later, eager to snoop through my mother's stuff.

"Dad, look!"

I had found an old foot locker in the attic. It had been my father's when he was on the road. Now it was cluttered, full of memories. Amongst the tattered trunk's contents were old *Les Miz* playbills, my and Sibby's birth certificates, and pictures of my sister, mother and dad at the Chicago blues festival.

"Holy shit," my dad exhaled as he momentarily took in the fond memories. "That old bag kept everything." He couldn't stay kind for more than a moment. "You know, this house is worth money," he said to me, as if I should be able to deduce what he meant by that.

"OK," I replied blankly.

"You should sell it."

I hadn't known that it was mine to sell.

"You and Sibby were her only kin. You should sell this piece of shit. Make some money."

My mind began to race. How much would this house sell for? $80,000? I could possibly make $40,000!? I was suddenly very glad I'd decided to come home.

I opened the phone book on top of the stack of phone books my mother was using as a living room end table and called the first probate lawyer I found.

"You'll have to empty out the house to sell it," he informed me.

Down the Rabbit Hole

There was no way I could clean out this mess in three days. I flipped to cleaning services and dialed 1-800-Got-Junk. Thirty minutes later they arrived with a dump truck. Three young, fit men in their early twenties entered the house. They stepped over debris carefully, as if the broken printer, empty detergent box and stack of old newspapers were valuable, and slowly took in the disaster that surrounded them.

"I don't think we can do this," one of them said. "We don't remove furniture."

Annoyed, but motivated by the possibility of making a large sum of money, I called out to my sister.

"Sibby! Come help me start moving shit out to the curb!" She did not reply. "Sibby!"

I headed down the hall. I heard sobs. She was sitting on the floor of our old room, crying.

"Oh, honey!" I cooed, bending down to embrace her. She hugged me back tightly, too tightly. She was angry at her mother for leaving her, and she took it out on my neck. "Ow!" I snapped, as I pulled away. "It's not my fault she died!" And just like that my sympathy turned to impatience and I stomped away.

The following day I got high in secret before my father and I returned to Bixby Street with a dolly. Together we muscled the washer and dryer out of the basement and up the small hill. My mother had collected old couches and chairs on the back porch and when we moved them, huge centipedes scurried from beneath, out of the sudden light.

"It's like she hoarded this shit on purpose, knowing we'd have to clean up her mess," I attempted to make light of the situation and bond with my father.

"I don't know how anyone could live like this," he replied.

Later that afternoon my sister returned. My mother's front curb was lined with furniture and appliances, yet her house still remained cluttered with trash. 1-800-Got-Junk arrived and got to work in the kitchen. Opening cabinets, they began throwing plates and glasses into heavy duty, fifty gallon garbage bags. Smash! Crash! Crunch! The sound of breaking ceramics was deafening, but satisfying. I felt relief and excitement at this house finally being empty. My sister, however, felt differently about the sudden invasion and destruction. She plugged her ears with her fingers and her eyes welled up with tears.

"Stop!" She shouted at the careless junkers who violated her mother's space. Turning to look at the emotionally unstable young woman who'd just yelled at them, the two men paused. "Stop throwing things like that! Don't you know? She just died!"

"Come on, Sibby," I comforted as I put my arms around her and guided her out of the house. "Honey, this has to be done," I explained to her once we were outside. I heard the plate breaking resume in the kitchen.

"I know," she replied, crestfallen.

"We have to sell this house and we can't clean it out ourselves," I continued.

"I know,' she repeated.

"It's all just junk, anyway, and I don't have time to go through it all," I kept on. I wondered if I was talking to my sister, or for the benefit of relieving some of my own guilt. But "I know," was all my sister said.

Down the Rabbit Hole

It took three visits, three dumpsters and $1,500 for 1-800-Got-Junk to clean everything out of Denise's old house. But when it was empty I felt elated. I brought over my father's vacuum, excited to finish the job. Alone in the empty house I'd suffered so much abuse in, I got high alone and smiled. I vacuumed each room, and felt useful, as if I had the ability to clean up the chaos my mother had left behind. I scrubbed the kitchen counters, and noticed the cracks and holes in the linoleum caused by years of neglect. Damage inadvertently caused by years of avoidance. One final walkthrough told me I was done. The house was smaller than I remembered. I wondered how it'd fit so much drama.

My mother's house sold for $64,000. Once all of her debts were settled, Sibby and I each ended up with $16,000. My father, being the lurker that he is, would drive by the house whenever he'd get the chance to see if he could sneak a glance at its new inhabitants. But, he said, it remained empty.

I'd never see the inside of my childhood home again in real life, but I'd dream about it a lot. I'd dream that Sibby and I would break in and take up residence there, making a lovely, bright new home for ourselves. The house is always well lit and clean in my dreams, the opposite of the way it was in real life. We'd fear the owner coming home at any moment, but he never would. As if he'd bought it for us. In my recurring dream our old, depressed house is repaired, and it feels as if my subconscious is trying to repair the structure and beams of my childhood. I've dreamt that I'm able to adorn the house with new furniture and throw pillows and leave it to my sister, and it feels as if I want desperately to be able to make everything better for her. I love these dreams of our old house because I like fantasizing that I am capable of repairing the past. That I can clean everything up and make it all better. That I can fix what my parents broke.

It's been eleven years since my mother died and eight years since I started working a program of recovery. In that time, I have forgiven her for the years of abuse. I see her more as having tried her best to be a mother, despite her diseased mind telling her that she didn't want to be one. I see that I was on the same path as she was. I understand her as having been sick, instead of evil. And I understand that she was in a tremendous amount of emotional pain that she tried to ease with drugs and alcohol. I know now that her anger had nothing to do with me, but was rather a by-product of her past trauma and alcoholism. It feels as if I understand her better with each passing day. Traits and thought patterns we have in common keep being revealed. Anger keeps getting replaced with empathy. I find myself identifying with her more and judging her less. And I honestly miss the good parts of her at times.

Down the Rabbit Hole

Chapter 60 — AA Crux

AA really ruins your drinking and using. Once you admit that you're an alcoholic to a room full of strangers, who have all admitted the same, you become a vulnerable sponge. You soak up everything you hear and no matter how much you drink or use after that you cannot get all of that AA shit out of your head. But for nine months I tried.

A week into my second purposeful relapse, I attempted to have my first (and only) one night stand. I met this guy on Plenty of Fish. We decided to meet at a bar near me. I was on my first martini when he arrived. He asked if he could get me anything. I said a shot of tequila. It was a large shot. I downed it. At some point he kissed me. I thought he was falling for me. But in actuality I think I was repeating myself and he sensed I was becoming easy. He wanted to go back to my place so we did and I attempted to fuck him. But, alas his penis was incapable of getting hard. He chose to ignore this fact, however, and attempted to proceed as normal, when I had a very sobering moment. *Really?* I said to God as this stranger attempted to penetrate my dry vagina with his flaccid dick. *Is this what my life has become?* I told him to jerk himself off while I watched and examined my choices in life. Then he left and I never saw him again. Or maybe I did. I don't really remember what he looked like.

Down the Rabbit Hole

I think people come into our lives for a reason. I had been working at Abramowitz Deli for a few months and had begun forming a friendship with Emma, one of the other servers. Emma was awesome! I had heard from Chuck, one of the wine clerks, that she was sober, but she was still young and fun. She had a bohemian style like a flower child, but was bitchy like a mean girl. We quickly became BFF's when she joined my gym and we became workout buddies. After spin or boot camp we'd go out to lunch and talk. I told her about my life and one day she told me she'd been sober for twelve years. I was astounded. I had no idea she was *that* sober! I couldn't imagine how she'd done it. As if I needed God to beat this sign into me I continued to use for a few more months while the attraction to what she had grew. We'd go to bars together and I'd get wasted, trying to maintain the outward appearance of having fun, while she'd stay sober. We celebrated my birthday together at my apartment while I drank a bottle of wine and she stayed sober. It was becoming glaringly obvious that I had a using problem as I continued to imbibe while this stone cold sober person sat next to me. It was as if God put a picture in front of my face of the person I wanted to be. I just had to confront my demon. My glaringly obvious demon.

On the day of my last drink, I went to a show taping with some other people from work. Before the show we went to a fancy bar. I had been feeling an increasing discomfort with myself, and the combined twenty-one days of recovery I'd experienced months before, along with the example constantly set by Emma, played loudly in my head. We left the bar to go to the taping and found we were too late. The audience had already been let in and we were shit out of luck.

"It's ok, I'd rather keep drinking anyway," one of the other people said. "Let's go to another bar!"

"I can't drink anymore," I answered, fearing that I might actually mean that on a deeper, scarier level than just at this moment. "I'm gonna go home."

I wasn't planning on smoking pot that day, but because the craving had been set off by the one drink I'd had, and because my night ended earlier than expected, I broke my promise to myself and smoked half a joint when I got home. Alone, by myself, I got into bed around nine thirty and began to cry. I could not live like this anymore. I had to stop.

The next day I went to AA and I cried. It was a round robin share meeting and I used my five minutes to pour out all of the fear that was at the forefront. The fear I felt that I was going to change my mind and end up using again. The fear that I wouldn't be able to do it. The fear of the unknown. I was absolutely terrified. After the meeting, I invited Emma over. I packed up all of my paraphernalia: bongs, pipes, papers, stash boxes, leftover pot and alcohol, in a paper bag and called my friend Janie.

"Can I bring you all of my drugs and alcohol? I'm getting sober and I need to get rid of it."

"Of course!" she supportively cooed.

Emma showed up a few minutes later.

"How are you?" she asked as she entered.

"Not good," I began to cry again. "I have to change my life."

"Yeah, you do," she replied.

I told her how I'd gone to the meeting and showed her my bag of stuff I was giving away. Together we poured out the remaining Hennessy that Janie didn't want, and she gave me simple instructions for the rest of my life:

Down the Rabbit Hole

"I want you to wake up every morning and read a page out of the *Daily Reflections*. Then I want you to pray for the twenty-four hours ahead, then meditate for five minutes."

"Ok," I said.

"Go to meetings, get phone numbers and call people."

"Ok," I said.

"I'm proud of you," she said.

I started to cry.

Chapter 61 — Boundary Setting

'Snow is like a cock. It's measured in inches, soft to the touch, cums when you least expect it and never gets as deep as you'd like. Driving in snow is like eating pussy. If you don't slow down and pay attention you could slide into the asshole in front of you!'

It was the straw that broke the camel's back.

'That is a disgustingly inappropriate text to send your daughter.'

It was the first time I ever set a boundary with my father. I was not good at standing up for myself. I usually just took it or laughed it off. I was used to ignoring how I felt. But this time, at thirty-two years old, I said something. And it felt good.

Nothing for three weeks… We used to talk on the phone once a week, sometimes twice. He must've felt ashamed or at least embarrassed. He didn't know what to say. He couldn't say 'I'm sorry.' He didn't know how. After he felt the awkwardness had diminished enough, he tried to call. I didn't answer. The next day he tried to call again. I didn't answer.

Down the Rabbit Hole

I just couldn't do it anymore. I couldn't continue to ignore the crudeness of our relationship.

When I was a kid I fantasized about the day I could abandon my parents. Why hadn't I done that yet?

"Your deadbeat sister had the balls to ask me if she could move in next door again." This was how my father typically broached the subject of Siobhan in our weekly updates.

"Well, do you take section eight?" That was how I remained loyal to Sibby while ignoring the part of me that screamed at him inside.

Why am I trying to keep this relationship alive? I don't have to. That thought freed me.

Five years passed. I didn't miss him. I was relieved, actually.

"Can you send your father a Christmas card?" My AA sponsor asked me in 2016. Somehow my dad had ended up on my most recent 8th step. I guess I figured I'd wronged him by cutting off communication with no explanation... Although I knew, deep down, he knew why. *Think about it. What was the last communication we had?* I asked him in my head using

Down the Rabbit Hole

his condescending tone. But I knew my father and his twisted mind well. I knew he'd blocked any wrongdoing from his memory and would claim not to know why I wasn't talking to him anymore. After five years of convincing himself he'd done nothing wrong I was sure he believed it, so I sent him a card citing a fond memory of one of our Christmases together.

A week later I got a six page, typed, single-spaced, size eight font letter updating me on the past five years of his life. It was as if my lonely father got my card and ran upstairs to reply as quickly as possible.

> "… I am no longer working as a stagehand in New York, as ever since my last show closed, I have not been able to get anybody to hire me for any of the new shows that have come out and are currently on the street. The word apparently is that somehow, some way, in some fashion or another, I managed to piss somebody off, and the word got around; and, even though I know there is no such thing as a blacklist per se, if there was one, I suppose I'm on it."

Yeah. Why try and right your wrongs? Pretending you didn't do anything wrong is so much easier. That was how he operated.

He wanted to know why I hadn't spoken to him in so long.

Down the Rabbit Hole

> "Siobhan hinted that I had sent you something via e-mail that you thought was crass or in bad taste, but for the life of me I don't remember ever sending anything that I thought was too over-the-top in that respect; because, hell, I've never sent anything to you that I wouldn't send to any of the females that I still have on my e-mail list, and I don't regard real gutter humor as being very funny in the first place."

Amazing how far away from the truth a delusion can carry you.

I wouldn't go back to the relationship we used to have.

> Dear Dad,
>
> I "cut off contact with you" five years ago because of the sexual text forward that you sent me. I had no idea that that would be our last correspondence for five years. But it ended up being because you never acknowledged it and I didn't know how to acknowledge it beyond my initial reply. I stupidly waited for some sort of acknowledgement or apology from you, but got none. Then, after a year of no communication, you emailed saying, "If you ever want to let me know why it is you won't talk to me I'd

love to hear it. Otherwise have a nice life." So... that was that, I guess.

But really that text was just the straw that broke the camel's back. It connects to a larger issue we've never reconciled: my childhood ~ the years of physical, verbal, emotional and mental abuse I suffered at the hands of you and mom. I have so many questions about those years, growing up, where you two were drinking and using drugs. I wonder if you feel regret about abusing me? Or if you feel completely justified and have no remorse? If you wish you could go back and change some of your past behaviors? If there are specific instances you remember where you know, deep in your heart, that you acted out of line? And if you're sorry? I feel like the un-dealt-with past blurred the lines of what was an appropriate adult father/daughter relationship.

You said in your letter that you always felt that we had an open and honest relationship, but I didn't feel that way. How could I when this elephant in the room remained un-talked about? How could I just forget the past and move on like it never happened? Especially without knowing how you feel about it? I'd prefer to have an open and honest communication with you, but I never felt like I could be open and honest because inside I was still that scared little abused girl. Afraid her daddy will rage at her for bringing up taboo subjects.

Another thing that added fuel to the fire was your relationship with Sibby. Sibby has schizoaffective disorder as a direct result of having been fed drugs and alcohol in utero. You raised me with integrity. You taught me that if I made a momentary bad decision, and it ended up negatively impacting the rest of my life, I'd have to live with those consequences forever. For example, I know I was not a planned pregnancy, but yet you "did the right thing," and had me. One momentary lapse of judgement resulted in a lifelong sentence. So I wonder how you don't feel the same way about Siobhan? The bad decision to allow Denise to ingest drugs and alcohol while pregnant - multiple times - resulted in a developmentally challenged daughter: a lifelong sentence. To give up on her seems completely out of line with what I thought you believed. It hurts me because I can see that she's sick, not evil. I know she makes bad choices, but that's part of her disease. She's just looking for love from anyone who'll give it to her. You have said, "her only problem is she's lazy," many times, but that is not true. She's severely mentally ill. Of course she doesn't have a job. Would you hire her? Because I didn't feel like I could say that to you I felt like a yes-man who was passively supporting you when I really disagreed. It makes me so sad to hear of you and Sibby's continued bad relationship. I wish, as the healthier of the two, and as her father, you'd be the bigger person and continue to be there for her despite your past feuds. She's alone and I feel so sorry for her it breaks my heart.

I would like to work towards resolving and improving our relationship. But that means talking about these subjects. I want that open and honest relationship that you spoke about. But the only way we can do that is by resolving the past. I'm willing to "put in the work." I hope you are as well.

I love you.

XOXO,
Punkie*

A week later I got a typed, single-spaced, eight page, font size eight reply.

"... I had completely forgotten that incident you mentioned - and even today, reading the first line of it, I couldn't tell you the punch line or anything else about it. I never gave it a second thought, because I never regarded anything I ever sent as being all that raunchy or classlessly disgusting; and I certainly never thought that some joke that contained sexual references would offend you, since we had always shared whatever online humor came our way; and I also thought that you and I had always had the sort of open, communicative dialog which enabled us to talk more like friends than like father and daughter. In fact, I regarded you that way - as someone I could trust, to tell my troubles to, to confide in and unload on. Or, to put it another way, I saw you - and still do - as an equal once you became an adult, not as a child. The other factoid in this is, I never - and this I can say without any equivocation - never sent out any e-mails like that unless I sent them to most of the people in my mailbox; and that included Tanisha, Jill, my old girlfriend Tina, and various other ladies such as they, and I would never send out something that I saw as being overly vulgar in taste. I'm not defending myself here, you understand; I am only relating why I had no idea what it was you were mad at, and consequently saw no reason to apologize for it. In fact, it was only years later that, I believe it was Siobhan, who told Sookie that the reason why you were angry was because of some e-mail, and it wasn't until then that I remembered the - what I considered at the time - nothing little tiff that we had on the phone because of it. I did remember you say-

Down the Rabbit Hole

ing something to that effect, and I also remember my reply to you at that time, when I said *since when did you become pure as the wind-driven snow?* I remember those exact words, because that is one of my favorite sayings, and I use it at any suitable opportunity; but all I meant by it was, Kate, you're over thirty years old now, you're not some naive, sixteen year-old vestal virgin who's never seen a penis, so how on Earth could some harmless little e-mail type humor be any sort of big deal? For Christ's sake, lighten up. It was a joke. That's it. No more. If you don't like it, delete it and be done. Let's not throw away an entire lifetime on account of it, and also let's not contribute to the politically correct bullshit that now exists in this world we now live in, where everything everyone says to anyone about anything at all can be considered offensive!!! I know you live and associate among the California liberals, but you also know where I stand on those sorts of things. My attitude about this whole incident, then and now, was *chill out*. I have never had anyone else ever tell me to reel it in when it came to the sort of humor that I used to send over the Ethernet. If, however, you truly are offended by this sort of thing, I will send you no more. And if you want an apology, then I will apologize for whatever it was that offended you; but I also reiterate that I didn't ever think I was doing anything wrong in my mind. Hell, if I had, I would never have sent it to you in the first

> place. So anyway, that's my story and I'm sticking to it; and you can take this explanation howsoever you wish to; but this is all I really know to even say about the whole affair."

It's like a filibuster. So many words just to avoid "I'm sorry." On and on defending himself without even realizing he's doing so. I can tell he feels bad; he's just incapable of saying it. His long, run-on sentences read as a full conscience. I wish someone would tell him that apologizing without defending yourself builds humility. And he could use a healthy dose of that.

> "Now when it comes to discussing the darker realms of our more sordid past, and all of the shit that you admittedly had to put up with as a kid, I don't know if you believe this or not, but not a day goes by that I don't think back with regret to the way you were treated; and no matter how much I would like to blame it all on Denise, you are totally right and I deserve a good portion of the blame for that myself. Perhaps, at least in the beginning, I deserved even more of the blame, because, Denise being who she was, I should have seen it, known she was crazy and gotten away from her - and taken you with me, which I most likely could have done."

Down the Rabbit Hole

It took me a long time to see this paragraph. It was hidden beneath so many excuses. But, wow. That was very big of him. Then again, even crazy people make sense sometimes. And, although he admits regret, he still doesn't apologize.

> "... you're correct that I never did technically apologize to you for my part in your history of abuse. I just never knew that it was still bothering you, and if you had ever said - or, better, written me - something at any time, maybe we could've cleared things up better then. I'm sorry that it has taken this such a long time to come up to the surface."

So close.

> "... there is one topic that you discussed in your letter that I can't totally agree with you on. And that, as you probably know, is the subject of Siobhan. Look Kate, I know you mean nothing but the best in what you are saying here; and I also am well aware that you do have some valid points. Siobhan was abused in utero. Denise drank and did coke while she was pregnant, and no, I didn't do anything to stop her. Just for the record, though..."

Down the Rabbit Hole

Of course. I know by now that every admittance of guilt will be followed up by an excuse.

> "… Siobhan wouldn't even be alive if it weren't for me. Denise was going to have an abortion - probably because she knew at the time, even though I didn't, that it wasn't my child, and it is even possible she didn't know what color the kid was going to come out. Who knows with her? But anyway, in one of the few times I did stand up to her about anything, she got pregnant, and I said, no way are we going to kill our baby. You're pregnant, I have a job, and we can support another little one, so we're going to have the kid. Simple as that. So in case you were never aware of that fact, I've already done a great deal for Siobhan, even before she was born… And one more thing I wanted to mention when it comes to Siobhan and how she was abused in the womb; how do you know what sorts of drug abuse Denise was exposed to in utero by her hypochondriac mother Nana when she was pregnant with her? She turned out to be an evil, abusive, self-centered, maniacal scumbag bitch, but maybe it was not her fault. Maybe it was all on account of the pain pills Nana scarfed while she was carrying. And how about me while we're at it? You don't know my real parents. I was adopted. Maybe my mother was some kind of raging alcoholic herself, which was

why she gave me away. You can say that I have done some awful things in this life, but how do you know that any of them were my fault? It was all on account of the way I was treated before birth, so it is unfair of you or anyone else to hold me to account for any of the actions I may have taken in life. Look Kate, I don't believe any of that psycho shit, okay? But my point is, you can carry this liberal non-sensical *I am as God made me* crap way too far if you want to, and find a reason to excuse anyone for anything for almost any amount of time if you try hard enough. There just comes a time when people have got to be made to stand up and be accountable for their actions."

He thinks I don't think people are accountable for their actions, when I am trying to get him to be accountable for his. Seems like he does believe that psycho bullshit.

"… I want to state right up front that I am not saying or writing any of these things in anger. What I am going to say here, I want you to understand, I am saying with all love… I made a million mistakes when I was younger, and not a day passes by that I don't have many regrets. That having been said, I am not going to spend the rest of my life apologizing for something I may or may not have said or done when I was twenty-six."

Down the Rabbit Hole

I was really just interested in one apology and a more respectful, less aggressive future relationship.

As I should've expected, defensiveness followed:

> "One small aside that has to be stated here, however, is that, in case you forgot, I filed for divorce and left Denise in Chicago, and it was during the time she was out of the house that she began coming to see both you and Siobhan while I was at work, and was begging for forgiveness and asking for a second chance. I distinctly remember both of you girls *taking her side,* and saying that we ought to take her back and see if we couldn't work things out. If it hadn't been for that, I would have divorced her worthless ass then and there…"

Now Siobhan and I were to blame.

I just couldn't do it. It was obvious he was nowhere near ready to amend his behavior in order to repair and resume our relationship. He didn't know how. I did not respond.

Down the Rabbit Hole

I pray for my father each morning and evening, but I also accept that he is exactly where he is supposed to be. Maybe he is not supposed to learn humility in this lifetime. Maybe I am not supposed to get the apology I crave; the one **not** followed by a million excuses.

I hope one day my father and I can have an open, honest, communicative, respectful relationship. Because occasionally I do miss the good parts of him. I remain open minded. But I will also respect myself by keeping my boundaries.

Chapter 62 — What it's Like Now

When I was 24 years old I told my dad I had started seeing a therapist. "Why?" he asked. I thought that was a weird response. I wonder what he was afraid I'd uncover?

As of today I have been sober and working a program of recovery for 8 years. In that time I've learned so much, and yet it seems the more I learn the less I know.

I only really know my own experiences. I can only be honest and tell you my truth.

My hope is that you can identify. If not with the events, perhaps with the feelings. Maybe with the thoughts.

Every day I relate more and more to my parents. Turns out the apple doesn't fall too far from the tree.

I have bouts of depression that mirror my father's. The difference is that when I'm going through them I share about what's going on in my crazy mind with people I trust.

Down the Rabbit Hole

I sometimes miss using drugs and drinking. Nay - I fantasize about the good times, and I sympathize with how hard it must've been for my mother. I experience addiction as progressive, even in sobriety, and I get it. Sharing about my cravings with a confidant alleviates some pain and lessens the burden. I wish Denise had had a group she trusted to confide in.

I have moments of joy that I wish my parents could've experienced. Pure gratitude and satisfaction with things exactly as they are at this moment. These moments don't last forever, but I recognize them out loud to another person when they come.

It's lonely in my head sometimes. I tell that to a friend. I am honest, even when being honest scares me. I realize I am far from perfect. I am just trying, as hard as I can, to be the best me I can be.

Made in the USA
Middletown, DE
29 August 2020